PR(

Decatur,

M000166736

The United Religions Initiative
is not merely a concept. It is an experience.
An experience of the other. . . .

The simple trust is this:
that the world will be enriched
if people of religions and spiritual movements
find a way to be in collaboration in the future
rather than duplicate what has happened among
religions in the past.

The Coming
UNITED
RELIGIONS

William E. Swing

Episcopal Bishop of California

PROPERTY OF CPC LIBRARY
1994 Clairmont Road
Decatur, Georgia 30033

UNITED RELIGIONS INITIATIVE, San Francisco
1998
CoNexus Press, Grand Rapids

Copyright © 1998 United Religions Initiative

All rights reserved to United Religions Initiative
and CoNexus Press except by special arrangement.

Part II may be copied without permission but with attribution.

Publisher's Cataloging-in-Publication
(Provided by Quality Books, Inc.)

Swing, William E., 1936-
    The coming United Religions / William E. Swing. -- 1st ed.
    p. cm.
    Includes bibliographical references.
    ISBN 0-9637897-5-9

    1. Religions--Relations--Congresses. 2. Religion and ethics.
I. Title
BL301.S95 1998   291.1'72
                       QBI98-66854

For more information, contact:
    United Religions Initiative
    PO Box 29242
    San Francisco, CA 94129-0242 USA
tel. 1-415-561-2300 /fax: 1-415-561-2313 /
email: office@united-religions.org / www.united-religions.org

To purchase books, mail payment by check or money order in $US, or
call, mail or fax all credit card details, address and phone number to:
    CoNexus Press
    6264 Grand River Dr. NE
    Ada, MI 49301-5945 USA
tel: 1-616-682-9022 / fax: 1-616-682-9023 / email: conexus@iserv.net

In USA, pay $8.95 plus $3.00 for shipping & handling one book plus
$.50 for each additional book. Outside USA, pay US$5.00 for shipping
& handling one book by Global Priority Mail plus $1.00 for each
additional book. For information about quantity discounts on 5 or more
copies, trade sales, other arrangements, or other titles, contact CoNexus.

CONTENTS

FOREWORD

*The Most Reverend Desmond M. Tutu,
Archbishop Emeritus*

Our home is heaven where God is. On earth we learn how to discover home, and each faith leads its adherents homeward. We must learn here how to live together with those with whom we will spend eternity. How can we arrogantly claim that ours is the only way and not learn to remove our shoes as we stand on what others consider to be holy ground, where they catch their glimpse of the Eternal, the Inscrutable, the Holy, the Compassionate, the Gracious One?

May the Initiative described in this book succeed for the sake of all believers!

INTRODUCTION

The first glimpse of the magnificent pinnacle of interreligious activity was seen at the Parliament of the World's Religions held in Chicago in 1893. By present day standards of fair representation of delegates, it might have been wanting. But in terms of what actually happened, it was truly remarkable. Nothing like it had ever been seen before on a global scale: Religions coming together with a bold agenda for themselves and for the world!

In reality it was a mountain-top experience without a mountain. A living, interfaith substructure did not exist. On normal ground where the people of faiths lived, interreligious interaction was almost unheard of in 1893. Nevertheless, after 1893 the world knew that something transforming existed in the hearts of some leaders of faiths. A mountaintop could be seen in the distance.

One hundred years later, at the centennial of the Parliament, the picture had changed. Local interfaith organizations were springing up like wild flowers. International interfaith movements produced a growing infrastructure of gatherings and voices. Pope John Paul II had invited many religious leaders to Assisi, and they had begun to pray for peace. Married couples of different religions were discovering how to live together, and mixed-faith families became self-conscious realities. Interfaith chaplaincies emerged in jails, hospitals, and college campuses. Scholars of religions attempted to give definition to the inevitable theological challenges. A mountain rose up from the valley floor.

The mountain, itself, became visible. What is now missing, as the old millennium gives way to the new, is the sight of the mountaintop. Today where can we see the religions and spiritual movements gathered *atop* the mountain with the same majesty and permanence that presently exists in the substructure of interfaith life? The initiative for a United Religions intends for the whole picture to come together—mountain and mountaintop.

The effort to begin the process—an initiative that yearns for a United Religions—is no one person's genius or copyright. The seeds for a United Religions have been planted in the hearts of people of goodwill throughout the world, among inestimable numbers of people of all religions, spiritual movements, and ethical practices. These seeds have been growing for a hundred years, as the Prologue demonstrates. These seeds will come to full bloom.

This book is both presumptuous and humble. Presumptuous because it assumes that the day has come for a United Religions. Humble because the author is keenly aware of his particularities. A man. A Christian. A westerner. Thus, severely limited in envisioning a place that will be inclusive. No one can speak for the world of faiths. But someone must shout if there is to be an echo. I do believe that an echo will be coming from the indigenous, from women, from spiritual margins, from the restless pious, from children, from refugees of religious intolerance, and, at last, from religious leaders. All have voices needing to be heard.

It is utter privilege for me to be engaged in such a hope. I have an urgency because we are squandering the treasure chest of spirituality that religions could be offering to the world, if only they could grow beyond mutual intolerance and even hatred to a place of mutual respect and cooperation. That place would be a United Religions.

Proposals for a United Religions: 1893–1996

A Brief and Incomplete History*

- 1893: The World's Parliament of Religions: The idea of a united religions came along with many other proposals.

- Early 1920s: Rudolph Otto suggested the creation of an Inter-Religious League as a parallel to the League of Nations.

- 1930s: In his book, *The Religious Foundation of Internationalism,* Dr. Norman Bentwich called for a League of Religions and said the idea had a long history including such proponents as Leibnitz and Rousseau.

- World Congress of Faiths was founded in the 1930s by Sir Francis Younghusband, who wrote that "a religious basis is essential for the new world order."

- 1943: Dr. George Bell, Bishop of Chichester, facilitated the establishment of an interfaith committee to provide "an association between International Authority and representatives of the living religions of the world," and produced the Three Faith Declaration (Protestant, Catholic, Jewish) to be presented to the UN, but was largely ignored.

- 1950s on: Starting with Secretary General U Thant in the 1940s, every decade has heard a UN proposal for something like the United Religions.

- 1950s: World Alliance of Religions held some conferences.

- 1952: World Parliament of Religions was founded at Presbyterian Labor Temple in New York to establish a permanent group "to work with a permanent United Nations to stop war and the causes of war and to extend the more abundant life among all peoples on earth."

- 1960s–1990s: The Temple of Understanding held Spiritual Summit Conferences to parallel Summit Conferences of world leaders.

- 1961–1996: Won Buddhists of Korea: Prime Masters of Won Buddhism have presented an idea of a united religions to lead in solving the spiritual problems of the world.

- 1970s: Shri R.R. Diwaker, one of the founders of the World Conference on Religion and Peace, expressed the need for a "united religious organization of the whole world."

- 1986: A World Council of Faiths was suggested by Dr. John Taylor at a meeting of large international interfaith organizations at Ammerdown, England, but failed to gain support.

- 1993: At the Chicago Parliament of the World's Religions, the idea was proposed by Sir Sigmund Sternberg, Chair of International Council of Christians and Jews, and by Dr. Robert Muller, former Assistant Secretary General of the United Nations, and was endorsed by many others. The Council for a Parliament of the World's Religions later explored whether it could pursue the vision, but concluded that a united religions organization was beyond its grasp.

- 1995: Although its vision was not a united religions organization, the Peace Council was formed as an organization of internationally known individuals to work together and support each other's work for global peace-making.

- 1996: The San Francisco Summit Meeting for a Global United Religions Initiative approved the proposal of a united religions that would begin with the purpose of pursuing peace among religions for the sake the entire order of life. This United Religions has a target date of the year 2000 for its charter signing.

*This information is primarily from a paper presented by the Rev. Marcus Braybrooke in April 1996 at Westminster College, Oxford, at an International Interfaith Centre Conference.

PART ONE

The Initiative for A United Religions

CHAPTER ONE

Gathering Courage

I began a long and inward journey in February 1993. During a twenty-four hour period in my life, I moved from being a person totally uninterested in interfaith matters to a person totally committed to being a catalyst for the creation of a United Religions. No coaching or coaxing. No reading or hearing. Just a sudden realization that religions, together, have a vocation to be a force for good in the world. I dedicated my life at once.

What I did then was to speak with many international interfaith leaders who were already involved in various efforts throughout the world. The timid part of me hoped that there were already groups working toward a United Religions, and I would then happily assist in promoting their cause especially in context of the upcoming United Nations 50th Anniversary celebration. It was to take place in San Francisco in June of 1995 with a special worship service at Grace Cathedral where I had responsibilities. Instead, I discovered that many international interfaith movements had, years ago, pursued a United Religions but had abandoned the idea because it seemed impossible to implement.

If I were to pursue the creation of a United Religions that would, in spiritual terms, be somewhat parallel to a United Nations, I would do so with a sense of single-mindedness. When I first told my friends, not one thought that a United Religions could be achieved. No one advised it. No colleague made partnership with it. Most advised that it was too ambitious a vision, yet there was a glimmer of understanding in their tone and certainly personal encouragement from a few local interfaith leaders. That helped.

My second foray into the possibility met with almost the same result. I went back to San Francisco and, on the advice of one international interfaith leader, planned a youth conference which was to be held three days before the UN50th service, June 25, 1995, at Grace Cathedral. Rabbi David Davis who was on the faculty at the University of San Francisco was successful in securing that campus for us. In the two years of preparation, curriculum formation for introducing the United Religions Initiative to the 200 young adults from ages 18 to 25 was given to a member of the faculty of the University of San Francisco. Coming down the home-stretch he announced that the United Religions Initiative had been omitted from the curriculum and he had instead planned the conference on "Rediscovering Justice." Obviously, tension followed. What came out was a compromise that allowed a little time for the United Religions Initiative as a secondary theme. So with the participation of Archbishop Desmond Tutu, Nobel Peace Prizewinner, Betty Williams, W. Deen Mohammed, and others, and with the presence of international interfaith leaders from around the world, some headway was made for the initiative at that conference. Major credit is due to the interfaith leaders who traveled the world to be part of background URI discussions during that week.

The third effort was the June 25, 1995, UN50th worship service attended by 183 ambassadors of the nations. Obviously, the spotlight was on the United Nations. Nevertheless, the vision of a United Religions was introduced in the service. Overwhelmingly the diplomats from around the world exhibited excitement about the vision and spoke positively about the prospects at social gatherings during the next two days. They would gladly welcome an arena for religious diplomacy in the midst of intractable political hostilities that often include unaddressed religious dimensions.

In July 1995 I sat down with four or five local people to see if we had any energy left after our two years of UN50 preparation to go forward toward the vision. Charles Gibbs, priest at Incarnation Church, was clearly on board. Peter Hart had already provided a draft United Religions Charter that was only written to serve to provoke thought. William "Buzz" Nern was going to start to work to provide a tax-exempt status (501c3). And there were one or two others. No office. No staff. No board. No money. Just looking vastly forward.

Here I want to jump ahead and give special mention to the support from various interfaith leaders of San Francisco leaders, such as Ms. Rita Semel, the Rev. Gerald O'Rourke, Iftekhar Hai, Ravi Peruman, David Ponedel, Paul Chaffee, Sister Chandru, Amaghalila Das, and many others. They were responsible for the UN50th worship service of June 25, 1995. In the planning and preparation, we all became quite a community of caring for each other. After 1995, these were the people who shouldered the local interfaith witness that eventually became the first Board of Directors of the United Religions Initiative. There could never be a URI if it did not spring forth from a specific place and then reach towards all of the globe. The fact that URI now has strong backing from the religious, philanthropic, cultural, and private sectors of the San Francisco Bay Area is due to these local interfaith leaders.

In September 1995, Charles Gibbs and I flew off to New York where I addressed the Religious NGOs of the United Nations. Although a strong rebuttal to our efforts was given by an important international interfaith leader, a clear majority of those present showed enthusiastic support.

Next came the February 1996 trip around the world to meet with religious leaders. India, Pakistan, Egypt, Israel,

Jordan, Turkey, Germany, Switzerland, Italy, and England were the countries visited. Among the hundreds of interesting, relevant conversations: Mother Teresa, the Shankaracharya of Kancheepuram, the Sheikh of Al-azhar, Hans Küng, the Archbishop of Canterbury, Cardinal Arinzé, Rabbi David Rosen, Sir Sigmund Sternberg, Imam Bukhari, H.H. the Dalai Lama, the Orthodox Ecumenical Patriarch, Pope Shenouda III (Coptic Orthodox), and Pope John Paul II. At journey's end it was like everything else. Ambiguous! Certain leaders liked the vision of a United Religions. Others wanted to know what various religious leaders thought. Some were opposed to it.

The overwhelming realization for me was that if there ever were to be a United Religions, the impetus would not come initially from religious leaders. Each of them has too much stake in defending the unique faith tradition invested in himself. (Yes, most leaders were men.) Interfaith activity is seen by religious leaders as a young phenomenon that is demanding more and more time. The farthest vision operating among them was to send out small parties of scholars and clerics to probe and understand distinctions between their own faith and that of other traditions. That religions could come together to discover a common vocation in addressing the urgent needs of the world is an unfamiliar concept. Let me add, however, that I was deeply impressed with the spiritual sensitivity of the world's religious leaders, and the weight of responsibility that each one carries. They were certainly not opposed to interfaith initiatives. They are open to sane, inspired initiatives and are rightfully cautious lest they betray their heritage.

Two conversations meant the most to me in trying to gain perspective. The first was with Dr. Hans Küng in Tübingen, Germany. He most graciously gave me a morning of intense inquiry. Again and again this Roman Catholic theologian would probe looking for the essence of the United Religions vision. When I left, I found myself centered on the underlying conviction of Hans Küng's Global Ethic project, which postulates:

> No peace among nations without peace among the religions; no peace among the religions without dialogue between the religions; no dialogue between the religions without the investigation of the foundations of the religions.[1]

After weeks of living with these convictions I came to the realization that the one distinct offering of a United Religions would be the pursuit of peace among religions. Other concerns will certainly swirl around a United Religions but the pursuit of peace among religions would lie at its heart. Absolutely nothing could be wrong with exploring the optimum level of peace that could exist among religions. Hundreds of times since that morning in Tübingen I have tried to spell out my best sense of a United Religions. Here is the latest mission statement for me although I am sure to tinker with it further while many more voices than mine will be involved in drafting a final purpose statement:

> The United Religions will be the global arena for daily and permanent diplomacy among religions and spiritual traditions; founded on common values of sacred origin, bound by a global ethic, lived out in a context of sacred hospitality, aimed at the pursuit of peace among religions, and aimed at taking mutual action in the face of urgent global need.

The second important conversation on this trip was with a friend, Lord Runcie, the 101st Archbishop of Canterbury. What was liberating was to hear him wrestle aloud with the frontiers of Divine Truth that go beyond our belief system. Not so much what little we know, but how vast is all that we do not know about how God has been revealed beyond our language, history and culture, symbols, etc. He wasn't afraid or defensive but seemed to be an honest pilgrim in anticipation of greater awe in the face of unfolding glory. "I do believe that many paths lead to God and once at the throne, nothing there contradicts Jesus Christ," said he. Lord Runcie also directed me to the *Nostra Aetate,* the first words of Vatican II's "Declaration on the Relation of the Church to Non-Christian Religions." On October 28, 1965, Pope Paul VI proclaimed these words of *Nostra Aetate*:

> From ancient times up to today all the various peoples have shared and continue to share an awareness of that enigmatic power that is present throughout the course of things and throughout the events of human life and in which, at times, even the supreme divinity or the Father is recognizable. The Catholic Church rejects nothing that is true and holy in these religions, (and) has high regard for their conduct and way of life for those precepts and doctrines which, although differing on many points from that (which) the Church believes and propounds, often reflect a ray of that truth that enlightens all men.

Leaders of religion have infrequently ventured out on the volatile line that separates religions to make statements of affirmation and shared truth. It is the boldness and the humility of the statements cited above that give me hope for the future of the United Religions. People of faith can touch the line of separation and not die.

The findings that came from conversations the world over were not off-putting. Just a reality check to appreciate the degree of difficulty ahead. During the trip I was honored to be asked to present a paper on the United Regions Initiative at an interfaith conference in Oxford. When I finished, the same international interfaith leader who had earlier given a rebuttal to my talk at the United Nations did the same at Oxford. I fared poorly. Most of the hearers were unimpressed or downright turned off. Nevertheless, I learned a great deal about what is or isn't on target with the development of the vision to date. At the end I thanked the folks for their feedback and stated that regardless of lack of success thus far, I would stay with the vision and keep pursuing.

In June 1996, fifty-six people whom I had met along the way came to San Francisco to see if we could link arms and together, build the Initiative. One instrumental partner had arrived on the scene, i.e., the Weatherhead School of Management of Case Western University, Cleveland. Dr. David L. Cooperrider, Co-Chair of the Center for Social Innovation in Global Management (SIGMA) had read about us in the *Cleveland Plain Dealer* and offered to bring a team of people to help us design events and introduce us to leaders throughout the world. Our destiny changed dramatically. Their genius calls for an approach of "appreciative inquiry" which starts groups out on a basis of personal discovery and affirmation. In many ways they transformed us and continue to do so. No help was more important to us than the quality of spiritually alert people that SIGMA brought to our tables. This was the first clue that if there is to be a United Religions, the original impetus and expertise will have to come from fields other than religion. Left to their own devices, religions will not meet each other. But given outside assistance from multiple disciplines which are already functioning on a global basis and have learned to work around and beyond existing roadblocks, religions can move toward common ground.

The June 1996 conference met at the Fairmont Hotel in San Francisco for two reasons. First, that is where the Charter of the United Nations had been signed fifty years before. And they offered us attractive rates. Who were the "us" that was organizing the event and charging bills with no money in the bank? It was a few people in the Bay Area who gave themselves to this vision.

At the 1996 Conference everything changed. Fifty-five people from around the world pledged themselves to become

18

the United Religions Initiative (one person declined). Instead of focusing primarily on religious leaders, it was decided to aim first of all for the grassroots faithful. The hope was that momentum would eventually build until at last, the religious leaders would be more inclined to approach each other. By that time a common ground of spiritual values and principles could be discovered and could bring a sense of basic linkage.

Two additional principles were put into action. First, we wanted to make sure that the United Religions would one day have a healthy percentage of women participants. During my travels around the world it was abundantly clear that most religious leaders were men. If a United Religions is going to reflect the actual world of believers of all faiths, women will have to have rightful access to the table.

The second principle had to do with spiritual movements. A significant number of people in many countries of the world will now describe themselves as "spiritual but not religious." Spiritual in personal meditation practices, spiritual in terms of concern for healing or the environment, spiritual in terms of personal piety! Wanting not to widen the distinction between religion and spirituality, we decided to include both right from the beginning.

This was not only a profound and soul-searing time; it was also a time of giddy naivete. We rented an office, hired a staff, made plans for regional United Religions Initiative conferences throughout the world, and called for a first Charter Writing Summit at Stanford University in June of 1997. Not a cent in our pockets to pay for the meeting we were having. No Board of Directors. No management plan. Just fifty-five people in 1996 who were aimed at gathering sixty million people to be a United Religions by the year 2001.

No sooner had we set up shop than the negative response came flooding in. Placard-carrying folks picketed us. One group wrote that I was the anti-Christ. A national newspaper article was written to say that the United Nations and the

United Religions were out to create one nation and one religion with us in control. A leading international interfaith group wrote that they wanted nothing to do with us. Radio talk show hosts from Boston and San Antonio put me on their shows to mock our efforts. One religious leader, sympathetic to interfaith work, wrote to the Archbishop of Canterbury questioning whether I should speak on his behalf at an interfaith conference.

Here we were, heavy in debt, trying to open an office, attempting to put the rudiments of an organizational structure together, flying around the world putting on conferences and giving talks, inviting responsible religions and spiritual leaders to a Charter Writing Summit, and a host of religious people thought we were a menace. So we must have been doing something right! At no time did we lack for courage or confidence in the vision. We were mostly afraid that our debts might overwhelm us.

Four people worked in a tiny office. The Rev. Charles Gibbs, Executive Director, with Sally Ackerly, Paul Andrews, and Mary Ellen Blizzard. They were, up to then, the ones volunteering and offering leadership. That is where we started. For a brief time the only council we had was the monthly Host Committee made up of anyone who had heard of us and attended to find out more. This freewheeling management style soon gave way to an official Board of Directors. The Rev. Charles Gibbs has been the key URI person from the beginning in working with the Board, running the office, holding URI events around the world, and providing primary spiritual hospitality. More than an Executive Director, Charles has been the local and global driving force for the creation of the Initiative.

A key distinction has to be made here. The United Religions Initiative was always understood to be different than the United Religions. The UR Initiative is the temporary scaffolding upon which people can stand while building a United

Religions. A United Religions was the ultimate goal. Its structure and membership and practice would have to be determined at a later date by the widest constituency possible. The UR Initiative would be centered in the San Francisco Bay Area and would organize around by-laws, principles of management, and an expanding committee system. The UR Initiative was planned to operate until June 2001 when the United Religions would come into being.

Visions of a United Religions have been put forward for at least one hundred years. All of them have been abandoned against the offsetting power of ancient feuds, the proliferation and alienation of modern religious bodies, lack of funding, poor communication links, and historic events that took precedence. A few groups have tried to advance a United Religions and then backed away. Others speak about a United Religions but have not set about to do the necessary work.

Our present UR Initiative sees several factors contributing to this time as the optimum moment for the birth of a United Religions:

- The 50th Anniversary of the United Nations, celebrating the nations, struggling together for global good, while for those same 50 years the religions have rarely spoken to one another. This inability to work together suggests the moral bankruptcy of religions.

- The approaching millennium is creating a rising expectancy for a new spiritual paradigm that moves beyond the clash of faiths.

- On the threshold of the first global civilization, specific groups are crossing borders to meet with other groups to pursue cooperative ventures: financiers, information experts, astronauts, politicians, athletes—every kind of leader except religious.

- Possibilities of instantaneous communication: in former days it would have been impossible to link people of indige-

21

nous faiths with religious leaders of the East and West. Now it can be done in a matter of seconds.

- A growing impatience with religious boundary lines and a fresh sense that spiritual realities are available to individuals and communities here and now. People of one religious group are discovering something of the spiritual genius of other spiritual groups.

What is of utmost importance to the building of a United Religions Initiative is that respect for and contact with ancient religions must be maintained while at the same time modern spiritual movements need to be invited into the conversation. In every URI conference, mailing, or speech, our success will depend upon the genuineness of our hospitality to all. Every tiny step we make has to be in keeping with the prevailing spirit that is hoped for in a United Religions. This is the rightful challenge as we utilize an old-fashioned organizational structure for the Initiative, stimulate a futuristic structure for United Religions, and carry out new ventures throughout the world as our constituency expands. As Albert Einstein said, "You can't solve a problem on the same level that it was created. You have to rise above it to the next level."[2]

Originally I thought that the impetus for the coming together of religions would be finding a common moral voice and taking mutual action—without getting into the areas associated with spirituality: meditation, contemplative prayer, sacred writings, end-time hopes, wisdom, etc. But I no longer think that. If there is ever going to be a United Religions it will only happen because the Ultimate Ground of Being wills it. Doors will open and paths will clear through roadblocks if the Divine Spirit has a vocation for religions working in concert. A United Religions will either have a distinct spiritual momentum far beyond its own cleverness or it simply will not be. Removing the realm of spirituality from a United Religions would be asking it to function with two hands tied behind its back. Obviously, religions are not experienced in sharing and respecting each other's sense of the sacred. But if we can move to an optimum level in these matters, perhaps religions can offer the full treasure chest of spiritual gifts to the world instead of the religious hatred, domination, and violence that is all too often presented to the world in God's name.

Like the man who jumped on his horse and rode out in all directions, the UR Initiative took off: regional conferences in Oxford, New York, Buenos Aires, Johannesburg, Nairobi, Egypt, Bombay, Delhi, Venezuela, and East Africa. Speeches in Japan, England, Los Angeles, University of Wisconsin, University of Colorado, University of California, to numerous Rotary Clubs, civic groups, as well as the Human Rights Caucus of the House of Representatives on Capitol Hill. Newspaper articles in southern India, *The Christian Science Monitor*, *the Los Angeles Times*, and the *San Francisco Chronicle*. Local chapters springing up spontaneously in Europe, Romania, New Zealand, South America, Sri Lanka, and Washington, D.C. Religious monks and nuns—Jains, Buddhists, Christians, and Brahma Kumaris—praying for the URI on a daily basis. Letters streaming in from all corners of the globe. A Web page on the Internet. Youth events in several locales. Interfaith education curriculum for young children. We outgrew our office and moved to a much bigger space. A periodic newsletter and a journal were published. In short, it was an explosion. Handling all of this was a staff of four and a world full of volunteers. My wife, Mary, who traveled everywhere with me, still volunteers at least ten— and sometimes 30—hours a week. I, too, am a volunteer as I continue to function primarily as the Episcopal Bishop of the Diocese of California.

Being a Christian and sallying forth into the world of other faiths is having a remarkable effect on me. I have stood on a sandbar in India's Pamba River with 150,000 Mar

Thoma disciples, been with praying monks outside the palace of the Dalai Lama, sat near Pope John Paul II in St. Peter's Square, listened on the floor to the Hindu sage, Shankaracharya of Kancheepuram, celebrated Easter with His Holiness Bartholomew in the Patriarchate in Constantinople, respected the faithful prayers in Delhi's Jama Masjid Mosque, said my prayers at the Wailing Wall in Jerusalem, was welcomed by the Oomoto people in their shrine in Kameoka, Japan, sat in audience with the Prime Master of Won Buddhism, and on and on. These experiences have enlivened, not watered down, my faith.

This journey teaches much more about the magnificence of God than about the possessions and prerogatives of any faith system. Jesus said, "Before Abraham was, I am." (John 9:58) It is the "I am" of God that moves beyond time dimensions and beyond the cultural and spatial settings of our various religions. Exposure to the proliferation of faiths brings a humility to our own spiritual grasp that is somehow in relation to the overwhelming, inexhaustible glory of God beyond our grasp. The experiences of the other only energizes my faith in God through Jesus Christ in the power of the Holy Spirit.

There are great people and movements to be met on the interfaith trail. The North American Interfaith Network showed me what is already happening in our part of the world. The Community of St. Egidio in Rome hosts religious leaders of the world each October where, following the Assisi example of 1986, all participate in prayers for peace. This event and these people are breathtaking. Dr. Diane Eck of Harvard is an encyclopedia of interfaith information and insight. The Rissho Kosei-Kai, though a young Buddhist group, has become a world leader in interfaith work. The International Association for Religious Freedom, with its General Secretary, Dr. Robert Traer, does a remarkable job on behalf of people whose religious rights are threatened.

Marcus Braybrooke, of the World Congress of Faiths, is a central or perhaps *the* central person, worldwide, in gathering interfaith information and inspiring people to the task. Dr. Daniel Gómez-Ibáñez of the Peace Council has begun critically important work of peace-making in Chiapas, Mexico. The Council for a Parliament of World Religions, which was formed in 1988 to continue the work of the 1893 World's Parliament of Religions, produced the 1993 Centennial in Chicago. Now, under the able leadership of Jim Kenney, the CPWR is making plans for new dimensions with a December 1999 event in Capetown, South Africa. Juliet Hollister came from the farthest distance to attempt the greatest interfaith quest and has given us the Temple of Understanding as her legacy. And largest of all and probably the most effective of all, is the World Conference on Religion and Peace with its inspired General Secretary, Dr. William Vendley. And there are many more groups out there doing local, regional or international interfaith work. I run into these people throughout the world and have a growing appreciation of their Herculean accomplishments.

All of these international interfaith groups are being invited to help create a United Religions which would be of service to them for assisting the mission of each if requested. So until the year 2001, the UR Initiative will be one more international interfaith group, but it will disappear. In 2001, the United Religions that will emerge will be the product of people of religions, spiritual movements, ethical practices, and international interfaith movements. Is the URI in competition with the other interfaith groups, competition for turf or members or money? No. In truth, the URI is only intended to be "in business" until 2001. The others will be functioning, God willing, long after that.

Most interfaith groups have survived because of the work of volunteers, contributions from individuals and foundations, and, infrequently, financial gifts from various religions. Similarly, the URI receives its monies from individuals, mainly, and some foundations. There is no serious competition for money because each interfaith group has its own sources of funding.

Another aspect of the URI organization is to get to know people throughout the world by way of Regional Summits. These are held in order for people to have a UR Initiative experience, to raise up leadership, to build local URI units, and to enlist input to our crucial summer charter-writing sessions at Stanford University. The Rev. Charles Gibbs and the SIGMA staff fly to various countries putting on these events. These are not high-powered, with lots of people. Usually between twenty and eighty people show up, and we do a great deal of improvising. Nevertheless, spontaneity prevails, and we discover new depths of richness on each occasion.

The cornerstone events for these years of the UR Initiative are the end of June gatherings at Stanford University. Some 200 to 250 people from around the world meet each year to lay the groundwork for an official Charter of the United Religions. In 1997-98, twenty-one "research and development" groups around the world met regularly on the Internet to prepare for the next June conference.

One of these small groups is responsible for structure. What might a United Religions look like in the year 2001? A smaller sub-committee is presently working with a consultant, Dee Hock, to present a draft which will be sent around the world for millions to critique. Dee Hock, who helped invent the Visa Card, has a global system of thinking which is called The Chaordic (chaos and order) Alliance. Here is another example how people outside the realm of religions have so much to teach us. Instead of organizing from a hierarchy downward, authority is invested in the smallest local unit. Thus the organization will be non-hierarchical, decentralized, and subject to constant reform. The sub-committee on Organizational Design has the responsibility of presenting an organization model of the United Religions so there can be a global critique.

Another research and development committee is exploring an ethical code which all religions and spiritual movements would be invited to create and, eventually, to sponsor. The members of this committee have been deeply impressed with "Toward a Global Ethic," which was prepared for the Parliament of the World's Religions by Dr. Hans Küng. Explorations in this area will be central to the formation of a United Religions.

Like most start-up ventures, the UR Initiative has money problems. When the URI began in June of 1996, we were $50,000 in debt. By June 1997 we were $400,000 in debt. Obviously, we are making progress! In response, people are making pledges and many of them are for four years, or until 2001. Currently (July 1998) our pledges exceed our debts. And happily the Dean and President of a Cambridge, Massachusetts, seminary has left his position to become our Vice-President in charge of development. Dr. William Rankin will begin in mid-1998.

The explosion of events has far outdistanced the infrastructure needed to sustain a global initiative. So on February 2, 1998, the Board of the URI had an all-day retreat to radically expand the supportive committee structure. Truly we are "building the airplane while in flight." As I write these words I am keenly aware that we stand in the middle creating our beginning and living hopefully into a future that outdistances us by light-years.

Earlier I mentioned that on a winter's night in February 1993, an urgency and a vision for a United Religions sprang uncultivated out of my innermost heart. I had a demanding "day job" and really no time to embark on so radical a mission and departure from my expertise. Yet there was no choice. I had no hold on the vision; the vision had hold of me. There was only and always one question. "Do I have the courage now. . . to pick up the phone? . . . to tell the story? . . . to be dismissed? . . . to get on a plane? . . . to trust that the right person, the just right person will soon appear? . . . to run up financial bills? . . . to allow my faith to be challenged by faiths? Do I have the courage?"

These words from Goethe are true and living, I know.

The moment one definitely commits oneself, then Providence moves, too. All sorts of things occur to help one that would never otherwise have occurred. A whole stream of events issues from the decision, raising in one's favor all manner of unforeseen incidents and meetings and material assistance which no man could have dreamt would have come his way. . . . Whatever you can do, or dream you can, begin it. Boldness has genius, power, and magic in it.[3]

I do believe that millions of people are about to enter that boldness and create a United Religions. From now on, for all of us, it is a matter of gathering courage.

NOTES

[1]Hans Küng, *Global Responsibility*, Continuum, New York and SCM Press, London, 1991, p. 138.

[2]Quoted from a pamphlet, "A Call to Leadership," produced by Soul Source, Washington, D.C., 1996.

[3]Goethe, from the Prologue of *Faust*.

CHAPTER TWO

Do We Have the Courage to Curb Religious Violence?

In the early Summer of 1997, people who were soon to be ordained to the priesthood and diaconate in the Episcopal Diocese of California were gathered in an early morning worship service. A woman stood at the lectern to read the first lesson, Deuteronomy 13:1–11. Here are some words from that reading.

> If your brother. . . or your son or daughter. . . or the wife you cherish . . . or the friend with whom you share your life, if one of these secretly tries to entice you, saying 'Come, let us serve other gods,'. . . you must kill him; your hand is to be the first raised against him in putting him to death, the hand of all the people will come next. You must stone him to death. . . All . . . must hear of it and be afraid and never again commit such wickedness among you.

Having finished, she closed the book and paused. She was supposed to say, "The Word of the Lord." The people were supposed to say, "Thanks be to God." Every new theological school graduate in the chapel was quietly wrestling with the appropriate response. Is it indeed the Word of the Lord which commands us to kill our relatives who would entice us about the "foreign" worship of a god not called "Yahweh"? That liturgical pause, that grinding of the inward gears by a new generation of ordinands is a tiny moment that keeps getting magnified around the world in response to all of the killing done in the name of the ultimate One. How are we to respond? The woman finally said, "Here ends the Lesson." Although no response was called for, everyone blurted out, "Thanks be to God."

"Here ends the lesson." Is the lesson about killing those who do not have the correct name for God, actually going to end? That is at the core of the present moment, when interfaith dialogue is urgent. Not just popular, but *urgent*. Religions are multinational entities which transcend governments and nationalities. In former days maps could be made which colored geographic areas according to religions. The blue was Muslim. Red was Hindu. Orange was Protestant. Green was Catholic. And so on. Religions were tribal, geographic, predictable. The Holy of Holies could be understood according to the place on the map. But no longer. The global migration of peoples of all religions means the intermingling of all the gods and all the exclusivity of the various beliefs in one God.

Do the old lessons continue to be "the Word of the Lord?" Or at the millenium time do we now say, "Here ends the lesson?" Whatever the answer, certainly the stakes are extremely high. With Christians, Muslims, and Hindus each having a billion members, more or less, it is a central question whether our divine duty is to kill or at least dominate each other. How can any nation or groups of nations even faintly hope for peace if the religions that command the hearts of their peoples have a sacred commitment to exterminate or dominate those of other faiths?

"If your friend . . . secretly tries to entice you, saying 'come let us serve other gods'. . . you must kill him." In a literal way of thinking, this command could be carried out. For instance, the blasphemy laws of Pakistan would make it possible for this to happen. It is also possible to interpret this passage and similar passages as metaphorically. For instance, the enticing relative could be treated as if he or she were dead, or, perhaps, disowned.

Despite such harsh measures, the main point has value: Do not allow other reports of the Divine to tempt your worshipful heart. Or, as the first of the Ten Commandments says, "Thou shalt have no other gods but me."

Is any dimension of religion deeper than that? This is the first commandment according to Jews and Christians. It is not foreign to Muslims, or, in fact, to more than half the people on earth. Yet if billions of people from exclusive religions are commanded to oppose the godly claims of other exclusive religions, what hope is there for peace among religions?

In order for a United Religions to come about and for religions to pursue peace among each other, there will have to be a godly cease-fire, a temporary truce where the absolute exclusive claims of each will be honored but an agreed upon neutrality will be exercised in terms of proselytizing, condemning, murdering, or dominating. These will not be tolerated in the United Religions zone. The prophet Habakkuk speaks of a vision that will change the old order and usher in a new one. "Write the vision; make it plain on tablets so that a runner may read it. For there is still a vision for an appointed time; it speaks of the end, and does not lie." (Habakkuk 2:2,3) We are living through a time of testing the new vision.

How do we make the journey from a religious tradition that is anchored in blood-taking hatred toward people of other faiths and move toward a combat-free United Religions zone? For people with no or little religious background, this question might be incomprehensible. They can quickly hop from the top of one spiritual mountain to the top of another until lighting easily on a pinnacle of peace. Not so for those whose souls have been fed and hearts have been set ablaze by ancient faiths. Centuries of historic drama with all of the subterranean attitudes must be dragged into the modern light of day. Down near the core of such ancient faiths is an almost unconscious abhorrence of other religions because other religions revere other gods. Therefore the journey to a United Religions zone requires a deep transformation of the heart. Otherwise "you can't get there from here." In terms of logic, there is no way to arrive at a United Religions. Religions have fought each other for centuries and millennia. Inside each religion are groups that hate each other more than they hate other religions. And at the core of most religious practitioners there is an unmistakable command to avoid contamination of other gods, at least, and to kill advocates of other religions, at most. Plus, there is such incalculable proliferation of religions, that the challenge of gathering them together is more than daunting. The only way a United Religions can possibly happen is that peoples of religions will discover a sacred hospitality and tolerance in their heritage and discover a new heart as they come in contact with the soul-life of people from other faiths.

Up to now, most but not all religions have recognized their own uniqueness around the motif of war or violence. God was discovered as the Boundless Power that saved one's ancestors and destroyed one's enemies. The definition of God, seared in the experience of people of faith, was determined around the outcome in the battlefields of the gods. A high percentage of popular Christian hymns have a military motif. Is it possible, now, to come to a defining moment where the Divine can be discovered in peacemaking among the faiths?

The United Religions can only happen if there is a new revelation that can be found in the affection of faiths. Can a person of one religion care deeply for a person of another religions without committing blasphemy? Or, more positively, can a person actually know God better by coming into a sympathetic relationship with the beliefs of a person from another religion?

In February of 1996 I was one of three people preaching

in Southern India at the week-long Maramon, a mission revival of the Mar Toma Church. Three services were held each day with between 75,000 and 200,000 worshippers in attendance. Additionally, in the early mornings there were Bible studies, one of which I led. Never will I forget speaking to a small group of people who were slightly exhausted and sleepy at 7 a.m. on a humid sandbar in the Pamba River. Not aware that the microphone in front of me reached people in the jungle as well as those in my Bible study, I interrupted my lesson to tell about a long journey I had embarked upon, a journey to religious leaders of the world in hopes of setting in motion an initiative to create a United Religions. In an instant, the little Bible study turned into a wild scene of interrogative and declarative assertions. Hundreds of energized people with Bibles in their hands came hurrying out of the jungle. They had come together at the Maramon in order to excite a passion to go out and convert every Hindu and Moslem possible. And here I was stating that the religions, themselves, need to come together and discover a new level of interacting. This, clearly, was perceived to be a threat to proselytizing. It seemed to fly in the face of Jesus' last exhortation: "Go therefore and make disciples of all nations, baptizing them in the name of the Father and of the Son and of the Holy Ghost." (Matthew 28:19)

That instant was a testing and turning point for me. What do I really believe about the contradictions set up by Christianity's exclusive claims? There was no time for quiet reflection or counsel. Here was an aroused crowd demanding an instantaneous response, and it had better be Bible based.

The first thing that came up from within me was Jesus' summary of the law. "Love the Lord our God. . . and your neighbor as yourself." (Mark 12:29-31) Pursuing peace among religions seemed to me to be necessary in order to keep the second part of the summary. How can we possibly love our Hindu neighbors, our Muslim neighbors, our Jewish neighbors, without granting them some respect and some freedom to worship as they feel called?

Once Jesus was confronted by the question, "And who is my neighbor?" (Luke 10:29) His answer came in a parable about a man who fell among robbers, was beaten and left for dead. Two leaders of Jesus' religion passed by the critically injured man. But when someone from a different religion came by, he took pity. Then Jesus returned his own question: "Which one of the three was a neighbor?" (Luke 10:36) The obvious answer was: the man who showed mercy. This teaches me that the Divine gives greater merit to actions that spring from a caring heart than to the pedigree of any religious tradition. If there is an elevated sphere of mercy that transcends membership in religious bodies, why shouldn't the people of the world be able to gather around agendas of mercy or justice or care for the environment? A United Religions would be a community of religious neighbors.

Since my experience in India, I have often read our ancient Scriptures and been stunned by interfaith insights which I had missed. The most poignant was the scene in the Garden of Gethsamane when Jesus was alone at night with a few of his disciples. Praying. Grieving. Preparing. Then all of a sudden into the Garden burst a great company of men with torches. Men with dominion over the government, the military, and the religion. Quickly they confronted the tiny band of disciples with Jesus. (Luke 22)

In a flash one of the disciples grabbed a sword and cut off the ear of the slave of the high priest. That was understandable and predictable. Religions do that to religions. Hadn't our ancient people driven the Canaanites out of the land by the sword? Don't we celebrate that Egyptians died in the Red Sea? Wasn't the madness of King Saul due to his unwillingness to carry out Divine instruction to "attack Amalek and utterly destroy all that they have, do not spare them but kill both man and woman, child and infant, ox and

sheep, camel and donkey." Saul annihilated almost everything and everyone but kept the best of the stocks. Because
he did not utterly destroy, God inflicted him with madness.
So, in the Garden of Gethsemane, when the disciple pulled
out a sword and began cutting, he was honoring the oldest,
strongest religious tradition.

"Jesus said, 'No more of this.'" (Luke 22:51)

With those four words the old way of inter-religious
relationships comes to an end. It is our duty, from the
Christian perspective to discover what is the new way of
interfaith life. The United Religions is a global invitation to
all faiths to discover a new way of relating, beyond the
sword. A way of healing!

On Christmas Eve, 1996, I was impressed by the celebration of a significant Christmas moment of antiquity. Therefore I preached a sermon which included some of these
words:

"History tells us that, on Christmas day 1500 years ago,
King Clovis of the Franks was converted and baptized as
well as 3,000 of his followers. It was clearly a turning point
in European history with far-reaching significance beyond
Europe. At that Christmas in 496, the bishop who baptized King Clovis gave him a very brief sermon. He
charged King Clovis to 'Worship what you have burned
and burn what you have worshipped.' These words have
been hailed as words of religious greatness.

"Religion almost always comes packaged in a 'winner-
take-all' wrapping. Seven hundred years ago, Islam was
spreading toward Europe, and Christianity was beating it
back. Today gentle Buddhists and Hindus are hurling
grenades in Sri Lanka. Hindus and Sikhs and Muslims are
murdering each other in Jammu-Kashmir. Muslims and
Christians are killing each other in the Sudan. Christians
are killing Christians in Northern Ireland. And Bethle-
hem, at the Christmas season, is under the paralysis of

religious hostilities. When religions face each other, 'compromise' is a dirty word. Nations must deal with some accountability at the Hague or on the floor of the United Nations or in a Nuremberg Trial. But religions? Religions battle each other with inspired insanity and conscienceless ferocity, and still religions stay immune from any human reckoning. Historic religious reasonableness would applaud the Christmas charge of the year 496, 'Worship what you burned and burn what you worship.' The Christmas equivalent of 'Burn, Baby, Burn.'

"In San Francisco, at Grace Cathedral during this Christmas season, there is an opposite vision. It is a vision of the religions coming together on a daily, permanent basis in pursuit of global good. To address such issues as the environment, population, war, human rights. To see if we can find a common moral voice, take mutual action regarding urgent human need. To teach and learn about other religions in order to gain a fair perspective and appreciation for the truth that is in each. To be a counterpoint to religious bigotry. To form a United Religions which would, in ways appropriate to religions, parallel the United Nations.

"There will be no wholeness for the created order until there is peace among religions. Hope in the next year, the next century, the next millennium approaches the threshold of tomorrow and slowly dissipates. We know in our bones that we all live in Bosnia-Herzegovina. There, the Orthodox and Muslims and Catholics lived side by side for years. Then one night an intertwining string was frayed, yanked, and the whole fabric fell apart in a nightmare of raping, torturing, murdering, and displacement of families. 'No peace among nations without peace among religions.' Well, then, let's get started with a peace which would be a joy for all of the people. We need to start. Sometime. Somewhere. Why not here? Why not now?"

"At Christmas, God is not guaranteeing the superiority of any religion but is saying something about God. Allowing us to see God as 'a child wrapped in bands of cloth and lying in a manger.'

"A God of humility. Not a warrior or conqueror. Not striding across the harvest of life but content in a manger, as a tiny seed come aborning. Showing infinite patience, wrapped in bands of restraint. A God of humility.

"A God of Humanity and the Created Order. Not eschewing the world and its gravitational pull toward primal dust but embracing it, elevating all matter with infinite possibilities. A God who so loves the world. A God of Humanity and the Created Order.

"A God of Endurance. Not winning all to himself, herself, Godself, but enduring opposition, competition, demonic resistance at the lowest and highest and most intimate levels. Tenacious, unwavering. A God of Endurance.

"And a God with ultimate confidence for the end of time. Not an insistence on manufacturing a time-certain plan of success. But a trust that ultimately everything is in the hands of a loving Creator. A God with ultimate confidence for all time.

"1500 years ago at Christmas, the Bishop said to King Clovis of the Franks, 'Worship what you have burned and burn what you have worshipped.' The days of holy arson are going to come to an end. For the sake of all the children of the world we are going to learn a new way for religions to interact. Jews, Muslims, Buddhists, Hindus, Christians —all, *all* of us will learn to live beside each other. Everyone will be invited to bring their best, richest, deepest stories to the common ground. Once there, we will begin by bringing the story of God in flesh. A God of Humility. A God of Humanity and the Created Order. A God of Endurance. A God with ultimate confidence for the end of time.

'The angel of the Lord stood before the shepherds, and the glory of the Lord shone around them, and they were terrified. But. . . the angel said to them, 'Do not be afraid; for see—I am bringing you good news of great joy for all the people.' For all the people.

"Amen."

The question is: Do we have the courage to curb religious violence? The angelic answer is: "Do not be afraid."

CHAPTER THREE

Do We Have the Courage to Create a Global Ethic?

On a hard day in November 1997, faxes arrived on the desks at the Arabic-language daily *Hayat* in London and Paris. The authors reported themselves to be representing the Armed Islamic Group (GIA). The message said:

> We are that band, with God's permission, who kill and slaughter, and we will remain so until the word of religion has prevailed and the word of God is raised high. . . . Let everyone know that what we do in killing and slaughter and burning and pillaging is close to God. . . . We inform you according to our faith and our ways: no dialogue, no truce, and no reconciliation.

Many things about this statement raise questions and doubts. It was not verified independently. Could it have been planted by an opposition to draw ire against the GIA? Certainly it runs contrary to the Koran and to the faith of hundreds of millions of Muslims who abhor such action and who suffer from unfair accusations.

At the same time the actions were explicit. More than two hundred people, many of them women and children, were massacred the day before in the Algiers suburb of Baraki. Throats were slit, people were beheaded, pregnant women disemboweled, and young women were kidnapped to be sexual slaves.

In the face of such atrocities, is there a permanent repre-

39

sentative body of the world's religions gathered and ready to condemn these actions, to declare that these actions are, indeed, not in keeping with an understood religious code of right and wrong among religions, and to intervene in helpful ways? No! But what if that were possible?

A start has been made. Two powerful forces merged between 1988 and 1993 to concentrate on the possibility of creating an ethic which would spring from the world of religion but also be available, and perhaps applicable, in the non-religious world as well. Creating a permanent representative body was not the agenda. What was the agenda was a global ethic. Chicago and Tübingen, Germany, became focal points.

Chicago came first. The Council for a Parliament of the World's Religions began laying plans in 1988 for a centennial celebration of the seminal, 1893 World Parliament of Religion. Daniel Gómez-Ibáñez, Executive Director of the Council, recalls that

> We decided to focus on the encounter of religion with the critical issues. By these we meant the grave and widespread threats to the global environment; the grotesque extremes of affluence and poverty; the divisions that wound our human family, such as racism, inter-religious hatred, gender discrimination, tribalism, and xenophobia; and the prevalence of war, violence, oppression and injustice. We saw these primarily as spiritual problems. . . . They are all a part of a single problem: how to live together justly and sustainably, caring for one another and for the planet that nourished the community of all life. . . . We wanted religions and spiritual people to come to grips with their responsibilities in the face of these most serious threats.

Next, action came from Tübingen, Germany—independent but similarly targeted. In 1990, Dr. Hans Küng produced a manifesto entitled *Projekt Weltethos* (in English,

Global Responsibility; In Search of a New World Ethic). He began by recording:

> Every minute, the nations of the world spend $1.8 million on military armaments. Every hour, 1500 children die of hunger related causes. Every day, a species becomes extinct. Every week during the 1980's, more people were detained, tortured, assassinated, made refugees, or in other ways violated by acts of repressive regimes than at any other time in history. Every month, the world's economic system adds over $7.5 billion to the catastrophic unbearable debt burden of more than $1500 billion now resting on the shoulders of third world peoples.

At the end of that section Küng stated:

> This one world needs one basic ethic. This one world society certainly does not need a unitary religion and unitary ideology, but it does need some norms, values, and goals to bring it together and to be binding on it.

In time, the Chicago and Tübingen consciences met and began to collaborate. What if a global ethic could be produced? What if it could be circulated first among religious scholars and then among religious leaders? What if this could happen by 1993 and such a global ethic could be the major focus of the Parliament when it opened on August 28, 1993? This ambitious goal was agreed upon.

Another voice was also heard at this time. Professor Leonard Swidler of Temple University, Philadelphia, was one of the notable scholars who made an effort to draft the ethic that the Parliament and Küng hoped for. Dr. Swidler stretched the thinking even further. Just as the United Nations created the Universal Declaration of Human Rights in 1948, would it be possible to compose a Universal Declaration of a World Ethos? This aim suited the concerned parties. So the word *Declaration* began to be associated with global ethics, and was intended to parallel the Declaration of Human Rights.

In chronological order, two other crucial elements came into play. When no one had been able to compose a consensus-making global ethic, Dr. Küng was entreated to make the effort, and he did. When he finished, two people in Chicago, Daniel Gómez-Ibáñez and the Rev. Thomas A. Baima wrote a shorter document titled "The Declaration of a Global Ethic," which became an introduction to Dr. Küng's "Principles of a Global Ethic." Yes, the titles became complicated, as was the debate about the drafting process and contents. The resulting compromise at the Parliament's Assembly of Religious and Spiritual Leaders was titled *Towards a Global Ethic: An Initial Declaration.*

If the question was asked, "Is there presently a global ethic that operates with authority among the peoples of religions?" four answers could be defensible. Yes! No! Not yet! Never!

Yes! In September 1993 at the Parliament, affirmative signatures were affixed to the Global Ethic document by most of the 150 religious and spiritual leaders meeting in the Assembly. More than 200 scholars and theologians from the world's religions had been consulted over a two-year period of preparation. "A minimal fundamental consensus concerning binding values, irrevocable standards and fundamental moral attitudes" had been explored not only to find the existing bedrock of shared values but also to be the foundation upon which a fresh consciousness might grow, the emerging global ethic for a new world order.

No! The process that produced the Global Ethic was uneven and its contents were not discussed at the highest official levels of the religions. Some critics questioned separating the moral concepts of a religion from the sublime vision of a religion. Others thought that Dr. Küng had put too much emphasis on the human—"the *humanum,* what is good for human beings," as the criterion for a global consensus—and too little on sustaining the Earth.

Not yet! Right from the beginning there was no intention to produce a once-and-for-all ethic. Dr. Küng wrote ". . . we shall have other declarations which make the global ethic of the religions more precise and concrete and add further illustrations to it."[1] Daniel Gómez-Ibáñez wrote that

> It will have succeeded as an ethic insofar as it succeeds in inspiring, provoking people to think, and to think again, about their values, attitudes, and behavior. We offer it to everyone hoping it will not be a monument standing firm, but a river: ever moving, changing, nourishing, carrying away debris and with the possibility of leading people of all cultures and beliefs to a better, kinder world.[2]

Never! Besides the colossal weight of evidence that the world of religions do not agree on anything, there is the problem of whether or not ethics are absolute or relative. At the Parliament in 1993 sexual immorality was condemned. Arguments that followed along the lines of sexual orientation were clearly drawn. In matters of non-violence there were strong objections especially since the Koran allows punishment of wrongdoers equal to the injury they have caused. If the moral teachings of one religion differ from the moral teachings of another religion, there can, it is argued, never be a global ethic.

The United Religions Initiative appreciates the cornerstone that was put in place by Dr. Küng and the Parliament. Presently, there is a "research and development" task force within the URI which is building upon and expanding the Global Ethic work of 1993. Dr. Charlene Spretnak, a therapist and activist in the international Green political movement, is the Chair. In addition to the Global Ethic and the Parliament of World's Religions' forthcoming "Call to the Guiding Institutions," the task force is examining kindred efforts such as "A Call to Action" by the Commission on

Global Governance, the "Religions and World Order Statement" by Global Education Associates, and the Earth Charter Benchmark Draft. Hopefully, the results of the Global Ethic Task Force will someday be folded into the United Religions Charter. At a later time an expanded form of a freestanding document on global ethics will be published by the United Religions.

Personally, I offer two contributions to discussions of a global ethic. First, I think at this time it is premature to name any ethics work as a "Declaration" along the lines of the UN's Universal Declaration of Human Rights. The United Nations Charter was signed at its beginning in 1945. The Declaration came later, in 1948. Such a global Declaration springs up after the creation of a global organization. The UN stands under and behind its Declaration. If a universal Declaration of a Global Ethos is brought forth without the underpinnings of an enduring global institution, it will lack gravity and binding power. A Declaration is derivative. Its creation and its continuance must rest on an abiding, global institution and on global acceptance.

My second thought has to do with the crucial matter of finding a stable consensus among enough religions to establish a global ethic as a binding document, an acceptable ideal. The experience in Chicago of hurrying to produce a document that needed to be hurriedly affirmed before the religious and spiritual leaders left town was a difficult way to accomplish the task. What actually happened was laudatory and the results moved the pursuit of a global ethic much further toward completion. Nonetheless, it will be important in the future for various religions, together, to find a path leading to a permanent body that will always hold the possibility of reaching consensus—on global ethics or any relevant matter! The following is a suggestion for such a path.

A Path for Various Religions, Together

- In order for various religions[3], together, to address the agonies and opportunities of the coming age, the religions will have to agree on basic principles.
- In order for various religions, together, to agree on basic principles, a consensus must be reached.
- In order for various religions, together, to reach a consensus, an on-going forum of interfaith engagement must be established.
- In order to establish such an on-going forum, a fair and hospitable process must be open to all for its creation.

Today the United Religions Initiative strives to be this process. In the next few years the URI intends the process to lead to an on-going forum and a consensus about basic principles.

In the future the United Religions Initiative will become the United Religions and the path will exist for religions, together, to address the agonies and opportunities of the coming age.

Not only should a global ethic be established within an orderly process, the purpose for having a global ethic must be clear at the beginning. Why have a global ethic? What purpose would it serve? Here are five purposes that I offer:

I

The first purpose of a global ethic is to define the ultimate family. In a family each member is related to each other. When family members come to visit, they are extended honor simply because they are family. How wide does the definition of family go? To whom are we related? Who deserves the honor?

The Vietnamese Buddhist monk, Thích Nhât Hanh, writes:

If you are a poet, you will see clearly that there is a cloud

45

floating in this sheet of paper. Without a cloud, there would be no rain; without rain, the trees cannot grow; and without trees we cannot make paper. The cloud is essential for the paper to exist. . . .

If we look into this sheet of paper even more deeply, we can see the sunshine in it. If the sunshine is not there, the forest cannot grow. In fact nothing can grow. Even we cannot grow without sunshine. And so we know that the sunshine is also in this sheet of paper. . . .

And if we continue to look, we can see the logger who cut the tree and brought it to the mill to be transformed into paper.

And we see the wheat. We know that the logger cannot exist without his daily bread, and therefore the wheat that became his bread is also in this sheet of paper. And the logger's father and mother are in it too. When we look in this way, we see that without all of these things, this sheet of paper cannot exist.

Looking more deeply, we can see we are in it too. So we can say that everything is in here with this sheet of paper. You cannot point out one thing that is not here. . . time, space, the earth, the rain, the minerals in the soil, the sunshine, the clouds, the river, the heat. . . You cannot just be by yourself alone. You have to inter-be with every other thing. This sheet of paper is, because everything else is.

Thích Nhât Hanh uses the words *inter-are* or *interbeing*. His thought is akin to John Donne's in the poem, "No man is an Island;" akin to the Buddhist concept of dependent co-arising; akin to chaos theory. Everything is related to everything. Up to now, ethics tended to be based on the isolated tribe. The global ethic will have to be based on the interdependence of all life. This will define the ultimate, global family instead of geographic or tribal or religious families. And we will learn to live accordingly.

II

The second purpose of the global ethic is to soften the human heart. Once we have a law or a moral code, we have, indeed, defined right and wrong for ourselves. This makes for greater security. Also, it subtly encourages people to confine their instincts of goodness merely to obeying the law. However, the human heart has a capacity for caring which far exceeds the minimal constraints imposed by laws. Simple obedience does bring minimal civility and orderliness, but has a tendency to harden the heart by constricting the flow of compassion. Sclerosis!

Here I speak from experience of the Judeo-Christian tradition. Once the people of faith were delivered from bondage, their overwhelming sense of destiny was quickly tempered by the unifying and demanding Ten Commandments. The ethics implicit in those two tablets from Mt. Sinai have been revered for thousands of years. "The law is holy, just, and good," says St. Paul.

Jesus was quick to say "Do not think that I have come to abolish the law or the prophets; I have come not to abolish but to fulfill." (Matthew 5:17). His interest was that the new ethical code would exceed the commonly understood laws. Thus he made a long journey into softening the human heart about doing what is right. We turned moral thinking inside out, upside down, always getting on the wrong side of the established thinking. "You have heard that it was said to those of ancient times. . . But I say unto you." (Matthew 5:21-48) Then he proceeded to give a list of impossible commandments, lest anyone feel self-righteous. To a world that rewarded conquest, he said, "Blessed are the meek, for they shall inherit the earth." (Matthew 5:5)

"For the hardening of your heart, Moses gave the Law" was the insight of Jesus. The ethics of the religious tribe was secure in the minimal quality of interactions among worshippers, family members, and neighbors. But the Law reached far beyond acceptable behavior to aspire to its ultimate purpose of softening the human heart especially toward people in greatest need. "Owe no man anything but to love another, for love is the fulfilling of the Law," says Paul. The purpose of a global ethic needs to elevate us beyond contractual agreements to a softened human heart.

III

The third purpose of the global ethic is to journey farther toward the whole truth. In the world of inter-religious violence as with all violence, it is not enough simply to live long enough for a new day to dawn. Atrocities have a life span in whispers and vengeance which keep them going into succeeding generations. If the whole truth about what actually happened and why it happened is not brought to light, then we give destructive powers the opportunity of continuing the old dark story in our own day. But if the whole truth is told, it will be accompanied by the genuine feelings which, alone, can put a former wrong to rest. Feelings such as profound regret and shame, feelings such as acceptance and forgiveness.

As an American, I remember visiting the Atomic Museum in Hiroshima on August 8, 1997, which was the fifty-second anniversary of the bombing of that city. While watching a movie of the event, I felt deep remorse. Then the narrator of the movie said, "While we were involved in a war, America dropped an atomic bomb on us. We still do not know why they did that." My remorse transferred in one second to absolute amazement at the denial inherent in the narration. What about the rape of Nanjing? What about Pearl Harbor? What about refusal to surrender? What returned me to my remorse, later on, was hearing about a Shinto ritual, "misogi," a nightly act of purification. One Shinto minister stood under a waterfall each night for ten years to purify his country and the shrine from the abuses of militarism. The cold water running over the body was intended to restore him to oneness with nature. We who have dropped an atomic bomb need also to be restored. We all must journey further toward the whole truth.

Archbishop Desmond Tutu would not allow apartheid simply to be dismantled. He insisted that a "Truth and Reconciliation Commission" be established in South Africa. Nothing like this had ever happened but it is a model of the global ethic that will emerge. Tutu writes:

> Unless you deal with the past in a creative and positive manner, then you run the terrible risk of having no future worth speaking about. The past can have a baleful or beneficial impact on the future. South Africa will be seriously undermined if those who benefited from the obnoxious apartheid system, perceived as the oppressors, will not ask for forgiveness for the awful things done under apartheid and if the victims, the oppressed, do not offer forgiveness.

In the coming day of interrelatedness, there will be no such thing as a secret oppression that is forgotten. All deeds will remain on the earth like radioactivity in the earth. The only chance for freshness among religions will rest in their ability to return to the scenes of religious hurt and tell the whole truth. A global ethic will necessitate truth telling.

IV

The fourth purpose of a global ethic is to take healing action in the face of inter-religious divisiveness. A global ethic will require more than an open heart; it will require actions that close the gap of hostilities between religions.

In the early winter of 1998 when the United Nations lost patience with President Saddam Hussein's unwillingness to allow international weapons inspectors to visit all suspected armament sites, war approached. Air, ground, and naval units were deployed in the Persian Gulf, and the prospect of suffering was imminent. Two people came into focus for me in terms of the vocation of a United Religion, in terms of a global ethic that must be established among religions.

The first person was a local Muslim leader named Iftekhar Hai. He telephoned me to lament the prospects of Americans going back to a Muslim country and once more bombing children as well as pinpointed targets. Iftekhar made a suggestion. What if he were to bring one hundred Muslim children to Grace Cathedral in San Francisco to talk with the Christian children in their Sunday School? This happened. In the midst of a wrenching moment one small healing action was taken in the face of inter-religious divisiveness.

The other person was the Secretary-General of the United Nations, Kofi Annan. In a last-ditch effort at diplomacy before the war, he flew to Baghdad and patiently listened through the list of grievances until he could begin to negotiate the difficult issues. His actions are a preview of what must happen if wars between religions are going to be negotiated in the future. Yes, Kofi Annan functioned against the backdrop of overwhelming military might waiting to be unleashed. Nevertheless, the military might, by itself, could not negotiate the peace. It required a United Nations to send an ambassador of global ethics. Coordinated healing actions are required.

When there is a United Religions, there will be a cadre of reconcilers, conflict management teams made up of various religions, at work throughout the world. Young people of all the religions will be invited into healing action teams, and the global ethic will have energy and influence.

V

The fifth purpose of the global ethic is to find the highest moral voice. There is no problem in hearing the lowest voice. It can be heard as mobs in the Sudan or Sri Lanka or the Middle East or Kashmir incite by-standers to join in the persecution of people from other religions. What about the highest voice among religions?

The voice of Pope John Paul II is the most conspicuous, and he speaks for the largest religious constituency. But what about the voice that speaks not for one faith tradition but for numerous faith traditions, together? From them there has been mostly silence until this moment of history. In the next millennium the collective voice of religions and spiritual and ethical traditions of the world will be heard. So many people are waiting. Diplomats, geneticists, social service organizations, parents, environmentalists, and more. They wrestle each day with decisions that will determine much of the life of this planet. What they want and need is a thoughtful voice bearing the wisdom of sacred traditions. An authoritative voice that comes out of the refining process of religions dealing with religions about real life issues.

Today, people of one religion can do what they will to people of another religion and there is no mutual accountability. Bosnia might have a functioning International War Crimes Tribunal. The Nazis had to face the Nuremberg Trial. But religious atrocities? Religions are not now accountable to each other. So there is never truth about facts, repentance of wrongs, or opportunities for genuine reconciliation. Someday soon, that will change. The people of religion, people who must worship because it is in their being, people of religion will discover that their voice is needed. A global ethic will express this highest voice.

At the end of 1997 in Baraki, a suburb of Algiers, over 200 people were massacred. There was no permanent representative body of the world's religions that could condemn these actions taken "with God's permission." That will change when we define the ultimate family, soften the human heart, journey toward the whole truth, take a healing action, and find our highest voice. Then we will have a global ethic of the United Religions. The question remains, "Do we have the courage to create a Global Ethic?"

NOTES

[1] *A Global Ethic*, p. 9

[2] "Moving Toward a Global Ethic," in *A SourceBook for Earth's Community of Religions*, ed. Joel Beversluis, Grand Rapids: 1995, CoNexus Press, p. 130.

[3] "Religions" refers to leaders and/or members of religious, spiritual or ethical organizations or practices.

CHAPTER FOUR

Do We Have the Courage to Embrace the Sacred?

I have a friend, Doug Bailey, who lives in Memphis, Tennessee. When the aorta artery in his heart had to be replaced, those near to him offered prayers. A five-year old boy named Davis was one such person. He was talking with his grandmother and this is what transpired.

Davis: "Grandmother, we've got to pray for Doug."

Grandmother: "Yes, you're right. Let's do that."

Davis: "OK, let's bow our heads."

Silence for several minutes.

Davis: "Amen."

Grandmother: "Yes, Davis, 'Amen.' But what about the words?"

Davis: "Oh, Grandmother, God knows all the words."

Many of the elements that I imagine in the United Religions' embrace of the sacred can be found in this brief exchange: Earnest intention around a critical human condition. Spontaneous participation! Trust in the Ultimate Mystery! Outrageous confidence! Even the young tapping into the deepest and dearest resources of the elderly!

Interfaith thinking and activity at a global level is young, even though there are examples of a few conspicuous interfaith voices and deeds during the past century. When I traveled the world listening to leaders of large religious bodies, it was impressive to hear for how few years anyone or any religious body had been engaged in serious interfaith exchanges. Five years is a typical number. Thirty years for a few old timers.

The global phenomenon of interfaith hope rides in the wake of a spiritual bankruptcy that pervades much of today's world's endeavors. Religion had a place of world prominence until it was dethroned in the past two hundred years. As Charlene Spretnak said in her article "The Spiritual Dimension of New Thinking About Development":

> The final pillar of modernity, the Enlightenment, was so named because the philosophers and others claimed to be leading us from the 'darkness' of religion, community tradition, and ties-to-place into the 'light' of a mechanistic worldview . . . . [T]he big players in the 'liberated' global market today are causing so much destruction to peoples, families, and communities that surely the anti-spiritual, economic-expansionist trajectory of the modern age must be judged a failure in many crucial aspects. It was a flight from wisdom in favor of knowledge for manipulation.

So religion returns for another hearing. Obviously religion never left the field of human endeavor. The worldwide membership in religions has grown considerably during these past two centuries and the influence of religions is pervasive at a core level. Nevertheless, hard-driving multinational companies and secular values promoted in movies, television, and advertising have isolated more and more people from the wisdom in religious traditions.

A revival of spirituality is in the air at the turn of the millennium. Magazines and book sales attest to the insatiable appetite of the public for literature having to do with spirituality. No particular religion is reaping the harvest of this attention because the focus is extra-religious, of a more diffuse spiritual nature. Cross-pollination of truths is available and sought out. Interfaith, which was the field of a particular few older voices, emerges now as a youngster, full of potential. A global "aching for God" is unashamedly laid bare. Interfaith is the child of the frustration with persistent inter-religious hostilities and the vapid interior heritage of our modern conglomerate gods. Individuals are making their way back to the Source by going around the embattlements of religions. Individuals are searching for the abiding values that elude the cults of popular corporate life. These individuals also constitute the young, interfaith longing that beckons to the religions for partnership, for an alliance that will lead to new forms of cooperation.

The full panoply of religious scholarship has not been unleashed on the emerging interfaith phenomenon but it is coming quickly. Annotated bibliographies of interfaith texts expand each month. The hard questions are being addressed in print and disseminated regularly. Where are the battlelines between the absolutists and relativists? Who are the saved and the not saved? What are the distinctions between the dogmatists and the mystics? How far is science from religion? Questions lead to sharpening of thinking. In the interfaith world the long march from vague optimism to well-defined understanding has begun. Hans Küng says "No religious dialogue without an investigation of the foundation of the religions." The investigation is upon us.

Many people start with the wisdom of a folktale. The Indian mystic Ramakrishna offered such help. He suggested that the aim of each religion was comparable to climbing the stairs of one's own house until at last one reached the roof. Once there, the person had access to the sky, stars, planets, the heavens. Others climbed the stairs of their own, thus different, houses, but once they reached the roof, they saw the same sky, stars, planets, the heavens. He went on to say that it made no sense to leave off climbing the stairs in one's own house to go to another's house. In the end the differences of the houses is irrelevant.

Theological inquiry goes far beyond such folk stories. Eastern religions, western religions, and indigenous religions pursue limitless aspects of the ultimate. In Christian thinking about interfaith matters, one central question is this: if a believer begins to demonstrate profound respect for the religions of others is the believer compromising the salvation and the faith assumptions about Jesus Christ and the Trinity? Initial answers to these questions tend to fall into three categories: exclusivism, inclusivism, and pluralism.

Exclusivism rejects dialogue with other religions because, according to scholars of this thinking, salvation solely belongs to Christians. Inclusivism embraces dialogue with other religions because Christ is believed to be anonymously present in other religions and thus salvation and truth are tacitly available to them. Pluralism thoroughly embraces dialogue with other religions because each is seen as representing a valid path to salvation. Obviously these three definitions do not do justice to the sophistication of each developed position, especially the scholarship that has been advanced on the third category, pluralism, by John Hick (*Guilford Lectures, An Interpretation of Religion*), W. C. Smith (*Towards a World Theology*), and Paul Knitter (*Toward a Liberation Theology of Religion*).

As a bishop of the Anglican Communion (Episcopal Church in the USA), I would like to give three examples from our tradition which roughly parallel these categories.

Exclusivism: Interfaith dialogue came into vogue shortly after the 1893 Parliament of World Religions. So when the Archbishop of Canterbury called together the bishops of the world to Lambeth Conference in 1897 the following resolution was passed:

> That the tendency of many English-speaking Christians to entertain an exaggerated opinion of the excellencies of Hinduism and Buddhism, and to ignore the fact that Jesus

Christ alone has been constituted Savior and King of mankind, should be vigorously corrected.

Inclusivism: In 1988, almost ninety years later, the Lambeth Conference passed the following resolution:

This Conference commends dialogue with people of other faiths as part of Christian discipleship and mission, with the understanding that

1) dialogue begins when people meet each other;

2) dialogue depends upon mutual understanding, mutual respect, mutual trust;

3) dialogue makes it possible to share in service to the community;

4) dialogue becomes a medium of authentic witness.

Pluralism: In 1998, Bishop Michael Ingham of Canada will go to Lambeth Conference buoyed in interfaith circles by the success of his book, "Mansions of the Spirit." He ends that book with a call for "grounded openness." By this he means affirming the sacredness of wisdom and beauty of other traditions while being firmly anchored in one's own.

Of course when a neat set of three categories becomes widely accepted, a host of people will want to expand to a fourth category. Scholars such as S. Mark Heim (*Salvation: Truth and Difference in Religion*) and Joseph A. Dinoia (*The Diversity of Religions*) do exactly that. Heim postulates that there are not just different religions; they are different kinds of religions. Thus all religions are not relating to the same Divine. Instead the religions are different systems with different ends, with alternative visions. Similarly Dinoia declares that the religions espouse different visions of life's ultimate aim. Since they all exist in widely different cultural settings, and have different theoretical and practical bases, they should not be compared as equal entities.

Reflections on the fourth option begin to allow for greater

latitude of thought and practice. For instance, key questions addressed by Joseph Dinoia suggest far greater freedom of considerations. Is it possible for non-Christians to be saved? Dinoia answers in the affirmative because the possibility exists after death. Is it possible for other religions to mediate grace and revelation? Dinoia answers in the affirmative because, since other religions have aims other than the Christian understanding of salvation, Christians could learn from other religions which pursue other aims. And finally, is there a sense in which Christians could affirm other religions as being true? Dinoia answers in the affirmative. His argument is that if a Christian accepts that the abundant providence of God is somehow behind the diversity of religions, then there is truth to be discerned in each.

Now the thinking moves into greater subtleties. A theologian friend of mine wrote a supportive letter to me about the United Religions Initiative and said: "When the theologians wade into interfaith matters, it will not be cozy." I suppose he is right. There is so much at stake here. Thus, there are so few benchmarks for helping us to move beyond anti-interfaith patterns of thought to more far-reaching possibilities. On the surface we seem to be making comparison about the superiority of one religion as opposed to another. In the end we will be talking about the nature of the Divine. How globally generous, how universally graceful is the Holy One? How expansive is the "embrace of the sacred"?

One approach that deserves attention is the approach of the Swiss author, Frithjof Schuon, in his book, *The Transcendent Unity of Religions*. Schuon does not consider the primary distinction to be between the religions themselves because at the heart of religions there is unity which transcends the world. No one can describe this unity and few people see it. Nevertheless, it is there. The important distinction is not between religions but between people within each religion. Schuon (following Huston Smith) draws a line through all religions as seen in the following drawing.

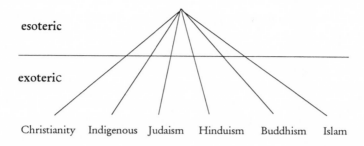

esoteric

exoteric

Christianity Indigenous Judaism Hinduism Buddhism Islam

Everyone above the line would be identified as esoteric. These people in all religions would intuit that they were ultimately in unity with people of other religions because all come together at the apex, in the Divine. Everyone below the line would be identified as exoteric. These people in all religions would wed the form of faith to the content or final truth of their own faith. Thus the forms of one's faith become absolutized because those forms, alone, are held to carry the truth.

When the esoteric and exoteric of one religion look at each other, there is bewilderment. The esoteric will look at the exoteric and applaud the investment in traditional sources of revelation, for example, Scripture or Incarnation. The esoteric will not, however, agree that the exoteric's insight is the only way in which the Ultimate Being has spoken.

The exoteric will look at the esoteric and have difficulty being charitable. The exoteric will tend to view the esoteric as a relativizer and a subverter of truth. To hold that God reveals truth to different people in different times in different ways threatens the absolute claims made by the exoterics.

These categories are helpful in trying to make sense in the world of interfaith dialogue. I remember being asked to do a live, long-distance radio program on a religious talk show of a large Texas city. When the two hosts spoke to their audience about the next speaker, they whipped the audience into a high lather by mocking some of the people who live in San Francisco. Then they stated that there was a conspiracy in the United Religions which aims at joining with the United Nations to form a single world government and a single world religion. Patently a fabrication, but by that point I was accustomed to outrageous falsehood. One interviewer asked me if there were only one way to God? I answered that there were many ways in which people have had a sense of the sacred, e.g., in the birth of a child, in a sight of nature, in a piece of music, in an enduring relationship. He began to scream so loudly at me that the owner of the radio station insisted that he come back the next day and apologize. Perhaps this was an esoteric/exoteric encounter?

In Old World thinking, a firmament (the ceiling of the sky) was over all our heads. Today, there are many people who are pushing at that firmament. It isn't that the sky is falling. Rather the sky is pushing upward and out. In the 1920s the astronomer Edwin Hubble announced that the universe was expanding. As of February 1998 astronomers using the Hubble Spacecraft have examined fourteen exploding stars (supernovas) at distances ranging up to ten billion light years away. One current theory gaining popularity in this field suggests that at the other end of the universe is an antigravity or repulsive force which brings an ever expanding universe. If the theological ceiling (the firmament) has been lifted, how far must theology or worship expand in order to begin to do justice to the Source of creation? Voices and hearts are pushing outward and upward following the embrace of the sacred. Here are a few such voices. They can sound like spiritual astronauts who have journeyed beyond our gravity's pervasive pull.

Paul Tillich:

> . . . in the depth of every living religion there is a point at which religion itself loses its importance, and that to

which it points breaks through its particularity, elevating it to spiritual freedom and to a vision of the spiritual presence in other expressions of the ultimate meaning of man's existence.

Dean Alan Jones of Grace Cathedral, San Francisco:

The fight is not between the absolutists and the relativists but between two views of the absolute. . . . There are absolutes that cannot be fully grasped or put into words . . . our struggle with language will never end. We are pilgrims of the Absolute. Some people are protectors of the Absolute rather than pilgrims of it. God doesn't need looking after. . . the Absolute exists not as turf to be defended or as proof of one's own superiority, but as the horizon toward which one is forever on pilgrimage.

His Beatitude Archbishop Anastasios of Tirana sees the Holy Spirit as the hope for moving into uncharted territory. He builds on the promise that "the Holy Spirit will lead you into all truth." Anastasios refers to

the Spirit of truth, working and inspiring human beings in their longing and in their search for truth in any religious setting, every aspect of truth, including science, related to human life. . . the Spirit of peace . . . helping to create new relationships among human beings, bringing understanding and reconciliation to the whole of mankind . . . the Spirit of justice giving inspiration and power for people to long and struggle for peace.

If the above mentioned "spiritual astronauts" are possible inspirations to a United Religions Initiative, if the theological thinking caused by vastly accelerated interfaith dialogue helps to launch a United Religions, then is it true that a United Religions would be another religion? Or a unit of religions which share common persuasions? Or a movement of esoteric people of all religions in contrast to the exoteric?

No, a United Religions can be none of the above if it is to

be truly a United Religions. In the same way that the United Nations is not a nation, the United Religions would not be a religion. Nor could a United Religions be the captive of western religions as opposed to indigenous or eastern religions. Nor could a United Religions be a battering ram for the esoteric against the exoteric or vice versa. A United Religions would have to be a level playing field, a well-honed balance among all of the religions and spiritual movements.

But what about the embrace of the sacred which all would hold in common as a bedrock assumption or assumptions? Although I cannot speak for all the rapidly expanding constituencies and individuals who will have input equal to mine, I will venture a guess that there will be two core assumptions which could hold all religions and spiritual movements together. Since we started this chapter with the outrageous confidence of a five-year-old boy in a godward direction, let me call these two assumptions the two unifying confidences.

Confidence One. *There is a Divine Unity at the center of the universe in which all life holds together. There is no place that is outside the sacred embrace inherent in this unity.*

When Magellan set sail to circumnavigate the world, he believed the entire world was one at the deepest level. So he sailed around the world without a map. Despite enormous obstacles he made his way around Cape Horn to become the first global citizen. Even so, a United Religions would be established on the confidence that the whole universe holds together in an ultimate unity and that unity is the sacred embrace at the core of the universe.

Confidence Two. *There is a kinship in the depth of all forms of life.*

It is right and appropriate to observe differences and to strive to survive. But, in addition to all that naturally separates, it is crucial that a search is launched to discover our relatedness. Therefore, words such as *hospitality, welcome,*

62

and *reunion*, family words, will have to be vastly expanded. The sacred embrace at the center of the universe creates a kinship which could be at the heart of a United Religions.

Perhaps these two confidences will be determinative issues for the United Religions' membership. If individuals or religions or spiritual movements choose to be affiliated, perhaps they could be asked to share in one or both of these confidences.

Here is another phrasing of the spiritual confidence at the heart of the United Religions. The unique aspect of these statements is the accent on the path rather than on the One at the end of the path. Perhaps this will invite more participation from more religions and spiritual movements. In the United Religions:

a) *Silent respect would be rendered to every religion as each pursues its sacred path.*

b) *That Which Binds Us Is Beyond Us.* As each religion renders silent respect to other religions, the rising mutual sympathy will lead to the discovery of a unifying mystery.

c) *That Which Is Beyond Us Will Bind Us.* The unifying mystery that will be discovered will persuade religions of an ever-increasing kinship with each other and with all life.

Here is the most delicate, dangerous, and promising aspect of forming a United Religions. Whatever approaches the sacred of any faith tradition runs the risk of inflaming hostilities. The time comes, though, when common language and a common purpose for all religions and spiritual movements must be discerned and agreed upon. Merely respecting and understanding other religions is not enough. Dialogues raise questions about ultimate belief. As religions converge upon each other in battlefields and grocery stores, classrooms and marriages, some common sacred sense must be discovered if we can ever hope for a modicum of peace. Kenneth Cragg said, "What has authority for some of the human race must have relevance for all." If the hot wires of all the

religions are becoming progressively intertwined and volatile, is it possible to create a fuse box? A United Religions
would be like a fuse box.

The United Religions would be like a . . .

1) *A positionless position.* The Japanese scholar, Masao Abe
wrote, ". . . there is no common denominator for the world's
religions. A positionless position makes other possibilities
possible through establishing a dynamic harmony among the
world's religions and opening up a dynamic unity in the
religious pluralism of our time."

2) *Going backwards in order to go forwards.* The United
Religions will not be a rejection of ancient religion but will
be found buried in the depths of these religions.

3) *One plus one equals three.* Rich, tough, transformative
interfaith dialogue is not a matter of pitting one religion's
philosophy against another religion's philosophy and ending
up with a satisfactory comparison and analysis. The best of
interfaith dialogue can end in mutual affection that goes
beyond reasonable calculation.

4) *A demilitarized zone.* The United Religions would be a
safe place where music, eating, child raising, playfulness are
possible. An Olympic village of the sacred.

5) *A spiritual refugee camp.* Throughout history people in
duress have taken sanctuary in monasteries because in such
places there was an abiding commitment to Divine presence
and expansiveness. Cultures that forbid prayer and meditation among peoples create refugees who walk until they find
a place that thrives on sacred meeting. The United Religions
would be such a refugee camp.

Since 1967, practitioners of Buddhism, Shinto, Christianity, and new religions in Japan have been praying and meeting so that someday "a framework of global alliance as a place
of trust and solidarity through spiritual exchange among
religionists the world over" would be actualized. Similar

sentiments are being expressed in Sri Lanka, Africa, the Middle East, India, Northern Ireland, and throughout the world. Their expression, their sentiment is the yearning behind the United Religions Initiative. Certainly, as one person, I do not have the answers to all of the seemingly intractable issues that confront the creation of a United Religions. But I do have confidence that the United Religions will happen. Like the five year old Davis who said, "Oh Grandmother, God knows all of the words," I believe in the silent embrace of universal sacredness in which a United Religions is being born. Nevertheless, the hard question must be answered around the world: "Do we have the courage to embrace the sacred?"

CHAPTER FIVE

...create new possibilities for the interdependent flourishing of all life

On January 20, 1948, an assassination attempt was made on the life of Mohandas K. Gandhi. Planned by Nathuram & Gopal Godse and a few friends, it failed. Ten days later Nathuram Godse did shoot Gandhi three times in the chest, a crime which led to his own execution. His brother, Gopal, was sentenced to life imprisonment. In 1967 Gopal was released from prison and in 1998, as the lone surviving member of the assassination plot, he had lived to see his dreams come true. The Hindu Nationalist party received the most votes in India's national election. Speaking from a long view of history, Mr. Gopal referred to ancient times when Hindu Kingdoms ruled India before Muslim invaders arrived. "It's been 1400 years. Finally we will have our Hindu Roshtra (nation)," said Gopal Godse. He and his brother wanted to punish Gandhi, a Hindu, because Gandhi backed the partition of Pakistan and was even-handed with Muslims in India. "Did I feel any repentance [for the assassination]? No. . . you see, it is not as if we had gone to New Delhi to steal Gandhi's watch. That would have been a sinful dirty thing. . . We killed with a motive, to serve the highest interest of our people," said Godse.

Here we have the ancient model of "un-united religions."

One religion comes into a country and dominates. After centuries the suppressed religion rises up and gets ready to dominate. If a leader tries to be even-handed with both religions, and seeks a negotiated peace among religions, it is permissible to kill him. The "highest interest" is the self-proclaimed right to dominate the society and the status of religion. This traditional form of un-united religions is entrenched throughout the world. Its life expectancy seems practically inestimable.

Where to look for an antidote? To the World Council of Churches? One must remember that the WCC aims primarily at one religion, Christian, and in that community, Roman Catholics and many evangelical and fundamentalist groups are not members.

To the United Nations? Although it does allow an increasing role for religious NGOs (Non-Governmental Organizations), it is clear that the voice of worldwide religion and spiritual movements is a secondary consideration at the UN.

If religions are ever going to learn to live together in a respectful way, they will have to step out of the shadows of their political, military, and economic allies and stand together on their own. It is so easy for religions, in the pursuit of ever greater popularity, to be co-opted by regimes that promise preferential treatment. If religions are ever going to learn to live together in a respectful way, they must call a truce in their efforts to annihilate each other and learn how to stand together in a way that doesn't compromise the integrity of any religion. No easy task.

Would a United Religions look like a vastly broader version of the World Council of Churches, only dealing now with multiple religions rather than one? Probably not. The core of the institution will determine the ultimate nature of the institution. While the WCC is unashamedly and rightfully Christian, the core of a United Religions would reflect that spiritual path as well as numerous other paths. Since the starting place would be different than the WCC, the organizational conclusions would also be different.

Would a United Religions look like a primarily spiritual United Nations? Perhaps. Can one imagine a United Nations without a peacekeeping army? Without economic sanctions? With conflict resolution employing spiritual resources? A United Religions could be what a United Nations can never become but what is deeply needed by the whole earthly family. It would be vain to wait forever for the United Nations to become what it cannot become, i.e. the global gathering place where religions can negotiate, share, and grow together as colleagues in serving the needs of the world.

A United Religions cannot be built by the United Nations; it must be built by religions. Religions will have to stop infantilizing themselves by "killing with a motive, to serve the highest interest." National destiny is not the natural ally of a religion; other religions are. A United Religions will invite religions to mature beyond the old promise of domination to the new promise of negotiation. Religions, together, have a sacred vocation. Yesterday that vocation always ended in murders and domination among the un-united religions. Tomorrow a way can be found to discover a United Religions which would unleash cooperation rather than fury.

What would such a United Religions look like? I don't exactly know. In 1945 the model for creating a United Nations was to develop a Charter, obtain a large piece of property, construct a large building, establish an Assembly and a Security Council, and live, day-by-day, through a bureaucracy. In 2045 that will not be the model of a United Religions. Whatever it is, it will be configured differently. But how do we begin to entertain new models?

One of the Research and Development task forces of the Initiative for a United Religions has to do with organizational structure. A consultant has been hired to help this task force create the necessary model of structure. Dee W. Hock, Founder, President and CEO Emeritus of Visa International, is that consultant. In his design for creating an organization, he is spending one and a half years with members of this task force to go, painstakingly, through six steps:

Purpose > Principles > People > Concept > Structure > Practice

Since this exercise has just begun and since whatever it produces will have to be critiqued by thousands of people before anything becomes official, there is no way to describe exactly what a United Religions will look like.

Understanding that the following statements are far from being official, they are mentioned here to give only a sense of the initial thinking in the task force and preceeding Summits. All of these could be changed; indeed, the June 1998 Summit endorsed a different statement of purpose (see the Draft Charter in Part Two).

An Early Proposed Purpose

The purpose of the United Religions is to enable enduring daily cooperation among the people of the world's diverse religious, spiritual, and ethical communities, to curb religious violence, to embrace the sacred, and to create new possibilities for the interdependent flourishing of all life.

A Few Proposed Principles

Principles of Practice

1) At the center of the United Religions is a profound respect for the sacred source and wisdom of each religion.

2) The United Religions offers a process of evolution for people of diverse religious, spiritual, and ethical communities moving from independence and competition to interdependence and cooperation, without losing the integrity of each.

3) Within the United Religions, conflict shall be con-

structively and cooperatively resolved without resort to social, ecological, economic, religious, or personal violence.

4) Individuals and organizations within the United Religious shall commit to being the change they wish to see, opening up possibilities for justice and peace in ways the world has not yet seen, especially in their home context.

5) While comprised of people from the world's religions, the United Religions is not now, and will never be, a religion. Instead, it seeks to honor the ancient and recent wisdom and good works of each.

6) United Religions' participants will not be coerced to participate in any ritual or be proselytized. All will be invited to learn from other faiths and share in spiritual exercises on a volunteer basis. The UR will seek to discover spiritual practices that will enable us, together, to honor and invoke the sacred.

Principles of Organization

1) Decisions and deliberations shall be made at every level by bodies (structures) and decision-making methods that fairly represent the affected views and interests, including those of women and children, and are not dominated by any single view or interest.

2) Throughout the world, the United Religions shall be open to all individuals and organizations (institutions) which fully subscribe to its purpose and principles, and demonstrate the commitment, capacity, and resources to pursue them constructively.

3) Each part of the United Religions shall have the responsibility to develop financial and other resources adequate to meet their needs, and responsibility to share financial resources to help meet the needs of all other parts.

4) All participants will have the right to organize in any manner, at any scale, around any issue or activity which is relevant to and consistent with the Purpose and Principles. The foundation of a United Religions is being laid from

the bottom up. What about the top down? At this point it will not happen that heads of religions would gather around the agenda of the United Religions. Until the grassroots is thoroughly launched and noticeably growing, it has only been important to plant the seed of the possibility of a United Religions in the minds of the religious leaders. And this has, to an extent, been accomplished. A large number of inter-religious dialogues, international interfaith movements, and Shinto, Buddhist, Jewish, Christian, Jain, Islamic, Zoroastrian, Indigenous, and Hindu leaders are aware of the United Religions Initiative. Now, first steps are in order. In the Fall of 1998 a small group of envoys of major religious leaders will meet for the first time together to explore how a United Religions agenda would offer promise for the world.

One proposed purpose for the United Religions includes *"to create new possibilities for the interdependent flourishing of all life."* The United Religions would not be intended to become a self-serving arena for religions and spiritual movements. The final reason to come together would be the ultimate enrichment of life.

Will the population problems of this earth ever be solved without the best wisdom, strength, and actions of religions working together?

Will the environmental problems of this earth ever be solved without the best wisdom, strength, and actions of religions working together?

Will the economic disparities of this earth ever be balanced without the best wisdom, strength, and actions of religions working together?

When one looks at the colossal nightmare of military weapons build up, one can hardly imagine regaining any global sanity without the voice of religions speaking together. My country, the United States of America, taught Iraq to make weapons of mass destruction to use on a neighbor. Later we almost bombed them because they could

71

make weapons of mass destruction to use on a neighbor. Multi-dimensional moral issues would benefit from the deepest wisdom that arises from sacred sources.

Letters now pour in for the United Religions Initiative to do something about one great modern issue or another. Free Tibet! Forgive Third-World Debt! Save the Rain Forests! And on and on. The desperate longing behind these pleas is for spiritual solidarity. As compelling as the issues are in terms of needing attention from religious bodies, 1998 is not a time for these to be addressed by the Initiative.

Please keep in mind that what is functioning now is the *Initiative* for a United Religions. The Initiative is not the thing, itself. Picture this. Building a large bridge across an enormous space. An ambitious engineering feat of the first order! While in process of construction, someone with an urgent human need entreats you to stop building the bridge above and in the meantime transport by boat, people that need to get across the wide river below. The primary task at hand is to build the bridge so that eventually there will be traffic and interaction and living possibilities that were, heretofore, unthinkable. Even so, the job of the Initiative is to build the bridge between religions. Someday there will be the bridge itself, the United Religions, which will, I believe, "create new possibilities for the interdependent flourishing of all life." At that time the issues will be addressed.

Even during this Initiative or construction phase, the mere news of a possible United Religions is a significant symbol of hope for people throughout the world. One example is a letter from Rohan Fernando in Sri Lanka. He related that years ago he, a Christian, wanted to marry Marji, a Buddhist. Because their families hated the religions of each other, they tried to poison the couple, lest they marry. Avoiding this threat Marji and Fernando were married, but at the wedding a fight broke out. Three people were killed and two were blinded. Then and there, the couple made up their minds that religious hatred had to stop. So they started an interfaith organization with a purpose akin to that of the United Religions Initiative. Today they have 1500 members but until now had no idea that this dream existed globally. So they wrote to the URI office, "How can we help?"

A growing body of literature throughout the world refers to racism and sexism. There is universal acknowledgment that hatred toward people of other races or discrimination against women is wrong, in Christian terms, evil. What the world fails to deal with is the unmitigated prejudice against people of religions. There is no such word as *religionism*, yet the reality is overwhelming beyond all measure. The existence of a United Religions will be a symbol that stands in direct opposition to the ancient, corrosive, and widespread hatred against religions that thrives, unchecked by religions. This global denial will end when the United Religions begins. Not only will the United Religions be a symbol of hope, it will also be a symbol that *religionism* exists and will be countered.

Create new possibilities for the independent flourishing of all life.

On Tuesday, March 17, 1998 in Kyoto, Japan, a unanimous resolution was passed by the Japan Religions Committee to endorse the United Religions Initiative. This followed an intense panel discussion led by people who had lived through the Atom bomb blasts of Hiroshima and Nagasaki. Out of the depth of great loss and suffering, a great hope arises. A mushroom cloud of hope that could fill the sky. These people have looked for a spiritual avenue for the world to pursue the sacred rather than the madness of conquest. Buddhists, Shrine Shintos, Secular Shintos, Christians and new religions aligned themselves with the Initiative.

Furthermore they volunteered to participate in the two major events on the URI calendar. On December 31, 1999 religionists of Japan will join the Religious Cease-Fire to pray, fast, meditate, repent and make resolutions for health among religions for the next century and millennium. Some of the Japanese expressed interest in visiting sites of religious conflict with others around the world on that day.

In June 2000 these Japanese religionists plan to walk together throughout their country and to sign the United Religions Charter. This is the first country in the world to make such a thorough commitment through its religions. Remember that in Japan the most destructive force of the last millenium was launched. Now imagine for a moment that it is the first place where the power of the sacred working among religions will be launched for the next millennium.

Truly new possibilities for the interdependent flourishing of all life can be seen on the horizon. Another example: Mr. Richard Blum of San Francisco took His Holiness, the Dalai Lama, to Jerusalem to meet one of the Chief Rabbis. At the start neither man was much aware of whom the other was or what authority he represented. Yet within a half an hour, the two religious leaders were holding hands and bringing prayerful blessings to each other. The surprise factor!

It is impossible to diagram the outcome of the United Religions. After saying everything that makes sense, the final appeal has to be to *the surprise factor*. In the work of the Initiative so far, there are numerous anecdotes about individuals of one faith encountering individuals of another faith, and the results are beneficial revelations to both parties. The United Religions Initiative is not merely a concept. It is an experience. An experience of the other. The result is the surprise factor.

The simple trust is this: that the world will be enriched if people of religions and spiritual movements find a way to be in collaboration in the future rather than duplicate what has happened among religions in the past. The desired nexus of collaboration can be the United Religions.

The path of Gopal Godse has been tried universally: "we

kill with a motive, to serve the highest interest of our people." This leads only to repression and is an invitation to vindictive counter-measures. As population growth and immigration patterns bring religions into increasingly close proximity, this path could eventually disintegrate into throbbing religious hatred as our daily diet—with no repentance!

The path of Gandhi, the path of fair-mindedness among religions has never been tried on a global scale. It is time to move beyond mourning his assassination to creating an alternative to religious blood lust and inflamatory rhetoric. This spiritual madness—whose first victim is the sense of the sacred—must stop!

The United Religions Initiative, its Draft Charter, Action Agendas, and the Global Cease-Fire present an invitation to pursue another attitude and to envision a new way for religions to be together. I do believe that a United Religions is coming and that new possibilities for the interdependent flourishing of all life will be created.

A Restless, Young Voice

The United Religions Initiative is a voice. A young voice. It belongs to coming generations that I can only vaguely imagine. It is the youth that have resonated with the Initiative right from the beginning and in the end it will be theirs.

The United Religions Initiative started with a Youth Conference in June 1995. Adults, prior to that Youth conference, did everything possible to keep this Initiative from the youth. During the Conference adults met early in the mornings and late at night debating whether or not a United Religions was worthy of pursuit. While the adults argued, the youths lived it. Two hundred young people from 46 different religions spontaneously walked to an open field, held hands, and prayed. They lived out something that adults could not work out.

In June 1997, I spoke to 1200 high school students (Rotary International Scholars) at the University of Wisconsin. My speech was merely an introduction to the United Religions Initiative. Even so, on nine occasions the youth began to applaud and twice there were standing ovations. I was blown away. The youth heard something in the United Religions vision that resonated with their secret and highest hopes.

My theory is that young people have already moved beyond the tribes that have so defined our theological landscapes. Their universe is vastly beyond our religious metaphors. It is as if they are in a larger universe looking back on our religious rivalries but they can not see our boundary lines. Why the senseless hatred in the Name of God?

When I travel the world, I am looking for a degree of

restlessness, a sense of urgency to get on with the task of religious peace-making. Among adults I see a deep satisfaction with the state of religion and inter-religious life as it now exists. Among young people I sense a readiness for building community among faiths.

The old millennium closes and I, as a senior religious leader, must listen. What I hear most compellingly is a voice, a restless, young voice. It sings in my heart as it yearns for a new time, a time for the Coming United Religions.

PART TWO

A Growing, Global Conversation

INTRODUCTION

by the Rev. Charles Gibbs
Executive Director of United Religions Initiative

The Benchmark Draft Charter of the United Religions Initiative is the result of a growing global conversation about the creation of the United Religions—a daily forum for cooperation and peacemaking among religions and spiritual communities. This conversation began in 1995 and has continued through countless gatherings all over the world, six regional conferences (Oxford, Buenos Aires, New York City, Johannesburg, Caracas, Nairobi), and three global summits in San Francisco (1996, 1997, 1998).

At this time, growing numbers of people, from over 50 countries and nearly as many faith traditions, are sharing their visions of how a United Religions could be a powerful force for global good. They are talking about the forces in our world today that are calling for and supporting the creation of a United Religions. They are discussing its purpose, foundational values, and principles. They are imagining a global organizational structure that encourages locally relevant action. They are exploring actions a United Religions might take.

This draft of the Charter is a first attempt to distill the vision, wisdom, and challenge of these voices. It was revised and affirmed for circulation at the Stanford 1998 Global Summit. It is far from complete, and will go through extensive development and revision between now and June 2000, when it goes into effect.

The draft Preamble, Purpose, and Principles are relatively

well-developed at this time. The Organizational Design section is a general sketch of an organizational concept and structure which will be developed extensively over the coming year, on the evolving foundation of the preamble, purpose, and principles. The Action Agenda section represents early thinking about potential areas of UR action in the world, and some proposed projects. This section will continue to be developed both as an essential part of the Charter and through pilot projects that begin to model the United Religions in action.

Many more spiritual and cultural perspectives are needed to bring the global yearning for a United Religions into full expression in the Charter. We hope that these perspectives come, from people reading and reflecting on this draft charter and from small groups of people all over the world attempting to live into the unprecedented interfaith cooperation for global good that is the goal of this initiative. Please join in this unique and vital process of charter development. You are needed. The Feedback section tells how you can help.

A word about language:

From URI consultations and conferences all over the world, it is clear that the meaning of words varies dramatically from person to person, from culture to culture. What speaks powerfully to one, seems trite to another. What is hopelessly general and vague to one, is open and liberating to another.

An example: in the statement of purpose that follows you will find the phrase "safe space." In previous drafts of the purpose statement, you would have found "permanent daily assembly" or "a common table." Which phrase communicates most accurately? To a certain extent, it depends on who's hearing the words.

This current draft represents a point in the process of seeking to find words that communicate a common vision in an inspiring, inclusive way. The words are imperfect, but they have been chosen carefully. Feel free to critique them, but before you do, live with them for a while in a spirit of openness and inquiry. For many people around the world they inspire a commitment to live into a new hope for the world. May they inspire the same in you!

United Religions Initiative Benchmark Draft Charter

for circulation from June 1998 through June 1999

Draft Preamble

We, people of many faiths, called by our traditions to compassion in response to the suffering of humanity and the crises which endanger our Earth community, wish to create a permanent forum where we gather in mutual respect, dialogue, and cooperative action to foster peace and the flourishing of all life.

We respect the uniqueness of each religion and faith tradition, value voices that value others, and believe that our shared values can lead us to act for the good of all.

We declare that our religious life can support us in building community and respect for one another, rather than dividing us.

We affirm that, in spite of differences of practice or belief, our faiths call us to care for one another.

We believe that the wisdom of our religious and spiritual traditions should be shared for the health and well-being of all.

Therefore, as communities of faith and interdependent people rooted in our faith, we now unite for the sake of peace and healing among religions, peoples, and nations, and for the benefit of the earth and all living beings.

We unite to pray for peace, to practice peacemaking, to be a force for healing, and to provide a safe space for conflict resolution.

We unite to support freedom of religion and belief and the rights of all individuals, as set forth in international law, and to witness together to the wondrous spirit of life which embraces all our diversity.

We unite in responsible cooperative action to bring the wisdom and values of our religious traditions to bear on the economic, environmental and social crises that confront us at the dawn of the new millennium.

We unite to be a voice of shared values in the international arenas of politics, economics, and the media, and to serve as a forum for research and excellence on values in action.

We unite to provide an opportunity for participation by all people, especially by those whose voices are not often heard.

We unite to celebrate the joy of blessings and the light of wisdom in both movement and stillness.

All members of the United Religions do solemnly vow to use our combined resources only for nonviolent, compassionate action. We devote our whole-hearted efforts to awaken to our deepest truths and to manifest divine love among all life in our Earth community.

Draft Purpose

The purpose of the United Religions is to create a safe space for spiritual partnerships in which the people of the world pursue justice, healing, and peace, with reverence for all life.

Draft Principles of Organization

1. We share a profound respect for the sacred source and wisdom of each religion.

2. We listen and speak with respect to deepen mutual understanding and trust.

3. We give and receive hospitality.

4. We address conflict through [practices of] healing and reconciliation, without resort to violence of any kind.

5. We seek and offer cooperation with other interfaith organizations.

6. The United Religions (UR) is a bridge-building organization and not a religion.

7. The UR welcomes as friends all who subscribe to its purpose and principles.

8. Deliberations and decisions are to be made openly and reflect diversity; they are not to be dominated by any single view or interest.

9. The UR honors, encourages, and depends upon local expression consistent with its purpose and principles.

10. The UR is decentralized. All local organizations have the right to organize in any manner, at any scale, in any area, and around any issue or activity which is relevant to and consistent with the purpose and principles.

11. Authority is vested in and decisions are made at the most local level that includes all the relevant and affected parties.

12. Each part of the UR has primary responsibility to develop financial and other resources to meet its needs, and secondary responsibility to share financial and other resources to help meet the needs of other parts.

13. The financial support of the UR shall be broad-based and reflect the UR's diversity. Deliberations and decisions on

financial support including contributions from donors will be conducted in a manner consistent with UR principles.

14. Every local UR organization shall surrender only such autonomy and resources as are essential to the regional and global pursuit of the purpose and principles.

15. The UR maintains the highest standards of integrity and ethical conduct, prudent use of resources, and fair and accurate disclosure of information.

16. The UR is committed to organizational learning and adaptation.

Draft Organizational Design

In two short years and with stunning cohesion, people on five continents have come up with similar versions for a new way of organizing. People from many different cultures and perspectives have envisioned a UR that is somehow inclusive, non-hierarchical, de-centralized, self-sustaining—one in which:

- resources are shared and decisions are made at the local levels;
- local initiatives are connected to one another for global impact;
- spiritual leaders of all faith traditions are revered;
- the deepest values people have are respected and put into action for the good of all.

We have shared a dream that an organization can exist in which ordinary people act from their deepest values and claim their right and responsibility to do quite extraordinary things to serve interfaith cooperation at a local and a global level.

At the URI Global Summit III (June 1998), delegates

engaged in a beginning dialogue about the organizational design that will be forwarded to an organizational design committee so that something much more concrete can be developed for next year's conference. However, even as a brainstorming session, there were two broad common ground conclusions by the thirty people participating:

1. The concept and structure of the United Religions organization should be a congruent embodiment of the Principles (as the Principles are improved and refined). We should not shy away from the challenge of inventing new organizational structures guided by the Purpose and Principles we believe in.

2. The structure and concept of the UR should be:

- Circular and networked (not pyramidal or command and control)
- Inclusive . . . made up of people of many faiths who share the Purpose (an organization of "we the people")
- Where local UR organizations are connected to regional/national associations and then globally

Various metaphors and graphics were offered:

- Indra's Net;
- interconnecting circles (with the "sacred" at the center);
- organic nature metaphors such as "a tree of life" with many diverse branches commonly rooted.

Draft Agenda for Action

(Condensed; the full text is available on the URI website, or through the URI office.)

Introduction

The United Religions believes that the purpose of human institutions and social systems is *Memayu Hayuning Bawono:* "to work for the safety, happiness, and welfare of life" (translated from the Javanese). This we interpret as enhancing and promoting well-being, spiritual development, and the Sacred within family, community, culture and the planetary web of life.

With this vision in mind, we commit to serving as *a moral voice and source of action grounded in contemplation* in each of the following areas:

I. Religious Rights and Responsibilities

II. Sustainable, Just Economics

III. Ecological Imperatives

IV. Building a Cultures of Healing and Peace

V. Sharing the Wisdom of Cultures and Faith Traditions

VI. Supporting the United Religions Agenda

I. Religious Rights and Responsibilities

The UR will take action to uphold religious rights and responsibilities. All religions and individuals have the right to freedom of thought, conscience, and religious worship. The world's religious institutions and the world's people have the responsibility to: recognize and practice the right to freedom of religion; practice and support all other human rights of women, children, men, and minorities; promote respect, justice, and solidarity among people for the good of all human beings and the earth. The United Religions seeks to uphold and support the Universal Declaration of Human Rights and The Universal Declaration of Human Responsibilities. The United Religions stands for the end of violence committed in the name of religion.

II. Sustainable, Just Economics

The UR will take action to meet the dire need to revisit the global economic system from a religious/spiritual perspective in order to make fundamental changes. To bring the moral voice of our sacred traditions to bear on the following issues:

- the present alarming rate of depleting the world's resources,
- the tremendous gap between the rich and the poor, and
- world trade that exists in arenas that are morally reprehensible and exploitative: the sex trade, the arms trade, and the drug trade.

III. Ecological Imperatives

The UR will take action to help humanity act with reverence for all life. We live in *an interdependent web of life;* all living things are both sacred and connected. Recent human activities, which have taken place in aggressive opposition to nature, have resulted in an *ecological* crisis. The root of the ecological crisis is a spiritual crisis. Just as the religions and spiritual traditions of the world teach respectful interaction with a sacred whole, so must spiritual values and moral imperatives help humanity to rediscover a reverence for all life and respect for the sacredness of the whole of Planet Earth. Therefore, we call for interfaith cooperation in furthering this vision for love and protection of the Earth, reverence for life, and harmony with all living beings.

IV. Nurturing a Culture of Healing and Peace

The UR will take action to nurture a culture of non-violence, respect healing and peace by working to develop a society in which all people can live without fear of violence in their personal lives, their families, their communities and their world. Nurturing a culture of non-violence means working to create a society that honors the intrinsic worth of each person, transforms suspicion into trust, and promotes healing within religious communities and the world as a whole. Securing peace should be a prime activity of the UR. The United Religions will become part of an international movement which fosters authentic personal and corporate good will and reconciliation, and which actively promotes peace. In particular, it will work to heal wounds by seeking tools from every faith for respecting the stranger, empowering nonviolence, and nurturing reconciliation.

V. Sharing the Wisdom and Cultures of Faith Traditions

The UR will take action to promote dialogue and a theology of acceptance to help the world's people explore common ground, awareness of unity within diversity, and ever-increasing kinship. Religion is concerned with the relationship of human beings with their spiritual Origin. We believe in the universality and eternity of the Spirit. We believe that all religions derive their wisdom from that ultimate Source. Therefore, the religions of the world share in common wisdom, which can be obscured by differences in religious concepts and practices.

VI. Supporting the Overall UR Agenda

The UR will take action to centrally support its overall work and its projects. A central office can serve as a clearinghouse to assist all parts of the UR by providing access to information, supporting grassroots efforts, inviting guidance toward enlightenment in a global voice, awarding recognition and appreciation to efforts within and outside the organization. And ensuring global distribution of financial and other resources.

Request for Feedback

What You Can Do to Develop
the URI Draft Charter

The URI needs to hear from a multitude of voices to help move our work towards developing the draft charter to the next level. Your own energy and commitment from the heart is what communicates and enlivens this charter document. We hope that you will share the URI with others this year according to your own ways; that you will enter into conversations about the Draft Charter; and, if possible, work with a group of people to live with the charter principles over the next several months. As part of the revision process, any feedback you gather is due November 30, 1998 and March 30, 1999.

Read and reflect on the Draft Charter using the following questions:

What inspires you about the Draft Charter? Why?

What is missing?

What are your suggestions?

How You Can Help

- Introduce the URI and this Draft Charter to people you think could help advance this work. Engage these people in conversation about the draft charter. Please send back key points from your conversations.

- Gather a group of interested people together and enter into conversation about the URI and this draft charter. (A Home Gathering packet is available to help this process.) Please send back the key points from your conversation.

- Take a further step and gather a group of people on a regular basis to launch a local URI group committed to living out the values and principles stated in this Draft Charter. Offer feedback based upon your lived experiences.

Your input is invaluable.

To give feedback on the charter and to communicate your efforts (big or small) to URI participants around the world, please contact:

The United Religions Initiative
PO Box 29242
San Francisco, CA 94129
Tel. 1-415-561-2300 / Fax: 1-415-561-2313
e-mail: office@united-religions.org
Website: http://www.united-religions.org

Your participation will help give birth to the
United Religions!

United Religions Initiative Global Cease-Fire

72 Hours Toward a Lasting Peace

The United Religions Initiative invites you to share in creating 72 hours of peace that will define a new hope at a critical moment in history—a gift of non-violence, peace and joy to the new century.

Background

Of the thirty-four wars going on in the world, religion is involved in virtually every one, a scandal that continues to undermine the spiritual message and moral credibility of all religious institutions. Religion has not only a calling but a clear moral responsibility to act for peace in these circumstances.

But religious violence is not restricted to places like Northern Ireland, Bosnia, and Sri Lanka. Those are merely the places we see its most bitter fruits. It is misunderstanding, ignorance, fear, and hatred that are the seeds of violence, and these seeds are to be found in our own home communities and indeed, in our own hearts.

It is time to change.

For too long, religions and faith beliefs have been used to justify conflicts and violence. It is the imperative of all religions and faith communities that their wisdom and power be used for peace and well being.

For too long, war has been considered an inevitable part of the human condition. It is the essence of all religions and faith communities to be peacemakers.

For too long, despair, cynicism, and apathy have impeded the ability to respond to violence and injustice. It is at the heart of all religions and faith communities to be bearers of hope, peace, and justice.

It is time, not just to stop particular outbreaks of religious violence, but to let go of the things that lead to such violence, and begin instead to sow the seeds of an enduring peace. Where there has been ignorance, to sow understanding; where there has been fear, to sow trust; and where there is hatred, to sow love.

The world we want will not grow of its own accord. We must plant the seeds, water, and tend them in order to create the harvest. Many people of faith are already at work in the garden. The purpose of the Global Cease-fire is to connect such efforts around the world, and to act boldly together to move beyond a culture of hatred and violence, and toward a culture of cooperation and peace.

A Call To Leadership

The ending of an old millennium and the beginning of a new millennium are fast approaching. Even for those who keep time by other calendars, this threshold offers a historic opportunity to reflect on our past and to move decisively toward a healthier common future.

With this in mind, you are invited to join with others in a worldwide act of solidarity in peacemaking: to reject the use of violence in the name of religion, and to plant new seeds of peace in the world, in our local communities, and in our hearts.

Accepting this invitation represents both a willingness to join with others around the world in a common effort, and a commitment to action within your spheres of influence over the months ahead.

What Will Be Done

From December 31, 1999 through January 2, 2000 (Friday through Sunday), the world's religious leadership will call for a Global Cease-fire—72 hours to work together for a lasting peace. Religious leaders will mobilize their communities for peacemaking, and will set an example for the world of how we can uproot the seeds of violence and begin to plant the seeds of a lasting peace. Leaders from other responsible areas of society (physicians, workers, scientists, farmers, educators, etc.) are enthusiastically invited to join in support and expand the solidarity in peacemaking.

To be part of this effort, you are invited to commit to—and engage your community in—the following:

- Participate in a worldwide, 72-hour cycle of continuous prayer, meditation, and silence by people of all faiths—to acknowledge the sacred, to ask for forgiveness and healing, and to ask blessings for all those who will live in this next millennium.

- Include prayers and blessings for those of other faiths in your tradition's religious observances during this 72 hours; and let other communities of faith in your area know that you are doing so.

- Commit to fast for at least one day during this 72-hour period—as a spiritual discipline, and as a way of declaring religion's universal concern for those who suffer.

- Support (directly or indirectly) groups of religious leaders who will witness for peace in specific zones of conflict during this 72 hours. We have already received four requests for such assistance from groups in Uganda, Sudan, Rwanda, and from UNICEF.

- Call together local religious and spiritual leaders to plan peacemaking acts at the local level (the URI can assist with the planning process for such gatherings).

To join in this effort, or for further information, please contact:
The United Religions Initiative
PO Box 29242 San Franciso
California USA 94129
Tel: 415-561-2300 / Fax: 415-561-2313
E-mail: office@united-religions.org
Website: http://www.united-religions.org